PLANET FOOTBALL

ANDREW GODSELL

Published in Britain in 2012 by Lulu

Typeset and design by Baby Alligator

Front Cover:
Lionel Messi playing for Argentina against Bolivia, at the 2011 Copa America. Photograph by Lgi Iz is in the public domain, presented on Wikimedia Commons, and used with the relevant permission.

Back Cover:
The author at England's match against Sweden in the 2006 World Cup finals – photograph by a bloke named Dave sat in the crowd.

ISBN 978-1-4716-1604-4

andrewgodsellonline.blogspot.com

The Author

Andrew Godsell was born during 1964, in Hampshire. His family owned land in the neighbouring county of Wiltshire – four hundred years earlier. After education at a nondescript comprehensive school and a sixth form college, Andrew did not go to university. He became something in the City, working for a series of banks, while launching a writing career. Following this Andrew has worked in public service, successively being a civil servant and local government officer.

Andrew's debut book, *A History of the Conservative Party* (1989), is a critical analysis of its subject. This was quickly followed by *The World Cup* (1990), a massive history of the world's leading football competition, and *My Life* (1991), the unique autobiography of a young author. After a spell in the doldrums, Andrew's writing revived with *Europe United: A History of the European Cup / Champions League* (2005), the most comprehensive chronicle of the relevant competition, and *Legends of British History* (2008), profiling famous events and personalities. Twenty years on from his autobiography, having reached maturity, Andrew published *Fifteen Minutes of Fame* (2011), a satirical commentary of contemporary society. Andrew's writings on diverse subjects have appeared in magazines, an educational textbook, and on several websites. Moving from fact to fiction, a contribution to textual accuracy led to an acknowledgement of Mr A Godsell in the Penguin Classics edition of *Dracula* by Bram Stoker.

Political activism has included participation in several General Elections, and even more local Elections, leading to a controversy with a Conservative Member of Parliament. In the world of very amateur football, Andrew played with more enthusiasm than technical ability for both Arab Banking Corporation and Deportivo Finance, before retiring from active involvement in the game. He was interviewed by the BBC at the 1990 World Cup finals, and ITV at the 2006 finals, but the film probably ended up on the cutting-room floor. Andrew's efforts have won table tennis and disco dancing competitions. He was publicity co-ordinator of Brooce Fans for Fair Ticketing, a campaign against ticket touting which attracted media attention. Following this Andrew featured in the book *Twenty Nights to Rock: Touring with the Boss* by Bill Tangen, an American sports writer, and fellow Bruce Springsteen fan. Andrew's supposed failings in domestic tasks have been discussed with amusement on ITV's *This*

Morning programme, and he has starred on the BBC's *Weakest Link*. Andrew lives in Hampshire, with his wife and daughter.

Contents

Preface

Football is a team game, but the brilliance of individual players is one of the most recognisable facets of the sport. This book profiles a dozen brilliant players of the modern – or relatively modern – game, with careers stretching from the emergence of Alfredo Di Stefano in the 1940s to the present-day genius of Lionel Messi. I do not suggest these are the twelve best players of their era, but amazing talent, combined with strength of personality, single them out as being among the most influential figures in the development of football. Having followed football since the early 1970s, I have been privileged to see seven of the players featured here in action, namely Johan Cruyff, Kevin Keegan, Bryan Robson, Diego Maradona, Gary Lineker, Eric Cantona, and David Beckham. Of the others, Alfredo Di Stefano retired when I was a toddler, while Pele, Eusebio, and George Best were playing, but past their prime, when I first became interested in football. I have just added seeing Lionel Messi play football to my list of ambitions.

If a bit of name-dropping is permitted, I once met the late George Best at a book signing event (for one of his books, not mine). I have also chatted with Bryan Robson, who autographed a match programme for me. In the lead up to publication of my book *Europe United: A History of the European Cup / Champions League,* the publisher negotiated with Alfredo Di Stefano to write a Foreword, but this did not materialise – so near and yet so far. Perhaps this book is an exercise in hero worship as well as football commentary. Hopefully I have been able to summarise the brilliance of the relevant players, sharing this enthusiasm with other fans, while adding fresh perspectives.

In the course of the narrative, I mention books written by several of the participants, plus other members of the football community, and take this opportunity to acknowledge the wealth of information found there. The researching of this, and many another book, has been accelerated by the magic of the Internet. I thank the compilers of the Rec Sports Soccer Statistics Foundation website, for sharing many, otherwise elusive, facts. Wikipedia is a massive source of knowledge, which I often make use of, and also acts as a gateway to even more online information.

Jeannette, my wife, and Anna, our daughter, have encouraged me in the writing of this book, and put up with my rambling about the inhabitants of Planet Football. I thank Jeannette and Anna for their support, and dedicate the book to them.

Andrew Godsell

Hampshire
March 12 2012

1 Alfredo Di Stefano: The Blond Arrow

Alfredo Di Stefano was the first superstar of modern football, building a massive reputation during the 1950s and 1960s. After success in his native Argentina, and then Colombia, Di Stefano crossed the Atlantic, and rose to new heights in the fledgling European Cup, scoring for Real Madrid as they won each of the first five finals. Besides goalscoring – his career total was more than 800 goals in first class matches – the strength of Di Stefano's game was the enormous scope of his play. Although he may be categorised as a deep-lying centre forward, Di Stefano ranged across the pitch. Helenio Herrera, an eccentric Argentinian whose path crossed that of Di Stefano several times in their careers, summed up the stature of the player with the following analogy: "Di Stefano was the greatest player of all time. People used to say to me 'Pele is the first violinist in the orchestra', and I would answer 'Yes, but Di Stefano is the whole orchestra'. He was in defence, in midfield, in attack. He would never stop running, and he would shout at the other players to run too".

The player explained his role in more prosaic, but equally enlightening, terms. Di Stefano anticipated the theory of "Total Football", which was to emerge a few years after his retirement as a player, with the following thoughts: "As a centre forward I am always on the move. Up, back, and across, trying not to be fixed in one position and so allowing the defender to see too much of me. Or I may be trying to avoid bunching with other forwards. Or I may be reading what is to come, and be moving quickly to help the next man on the ball. Forwards should accept it as part of their job that they should help the defence. When the opposing attack is in possession, you obviously are out of the game. What do you do? Just accept that position, while the defence tries to come through a difficult time? If the defence fails, the forward's job becomes that much harder. He has to score more goals. So the obvious thing is to get back quickly and help the defence. It eases your own job over the game. I think nothing of popping up at centre half or full back, to cover a colleague who has had to leave his position. We are all footballers, and as such should be able to perform competently in all eleven positions".

Di Stefano was born on July 4 1926, at Buenos Aires in Argentina, into a family of Italian immigrants. He had to work on his family farm as a youth, but this had the effect of building his strength and stamina. Alfredo joined River Plate, a club his father had played for, and made his first team debut at the age of 16. During his early years with the club, before he established a regular place in the team, Di Stefano was loaned to Huracan, but soon returned to River Plate, whose fans nicknamed him "the Blond Arrow", for his ability to dart around the field. Di Stefano helped River Plate to win the Argentinian title in 1947. In that year he also starred for Argentina, as they won the South American championship, which was staged in Ecuador, scoring six goals in six appearances. Apart from that tournament, Di Stefano only played one other match for Argentina.

In 1949 Di Stefano moved to Los Millionarios, a club in Colombia whose very name was chosen to symbolise its wealth. The Colombians had set up a rebel league, beyond the auspices of FIFA. The clubs refused to pay transfer fees, but offered high pay which led many South American footballers, plus some from England, to join them. Los Millionarios dominated the new league, while Di Stefano was even selected to play twice for Colombia's national team, on the basis of his short residence there.

Real Madrid arranged to buy Di Stefano from Los Millionarios in 1953, but at the same time Barcelona agreed a transfer with River Plate, who officially still held the player's registration. With Real and Barcelona in dispute over which club Di Stefano now belonged to, the Spanish football authorities arranged a compromise whereby he would play alternate seasons for the two clubs. Barcelona's enthusiasm for the player soon waned, and they agreed to sell their rights in return for Real reimbursing the paltry fee of USD 27,000 they had paid to River Plate. Di Stefano soon emphasised his real value, by scoring four goals as Real beat Barcelona 5-0.

The arrival of Di Stefano helped transform Real Madrid into a team that dominated the Spanish, and then the European, game. After many years in the doldrums, Real Madrid won the Spanish league in 1954, for the first time since 1933. Real had a fine manger in Jose Villalonga, but the revival of the club owed more to the influence of Santiago Bernabeu, who had been their President since 1943. Bernabeu had launched a membership scheme for the club's supporters – a novelty in those days – and used the proceeds to build a massive arena. This was opened in 1947, and renamed the Santiago Bernabeu Stadium in 1955. The investment paid off, with the revenues from large crowds financing the further development of the club, and fulfilling the dreams Bernabeu had for Real Madrid. During 1955, a year in which Real retained the Spanish championship, Bernabeu was one of the enthusiasts who did much to turn the idea of a European Cup into reality.

In 1955-56 Real Madrid won the inaugural European Cup. In the Final Real Madrid met Stade de Reims, at Paris. Reims scored twice in the first ten minutes, before Real Madrid got back into the game on the quarter of an hour mark, courtesy of a great goal from Di Stefano, who beat two opponents in midfield, exchanged passes with Marsal, and then scored with a powerful shot. On the half hour Real pulled level at 2-2. Reims regained the lead in the second half, but Real Madrid thwarted them with another fight back, and the Spanish club eventually won a thrilling match 4-3. Ironically Real Madrid's victory in the first European Cup Final owed much to the performances of two Argentinians. Besides Di Stefano scoring once, and inspiring the team's recovery, his fellow-countryman Hector Rial had netted twice in the match.

Real reached the European Cup Final again the following season, with their opponents being Fiorentina. Real had the great advantage that their stadium had been chosen in advance as the venue for the Final, in honour of the club winning the inaugural European Cup. Despite being cheered on by a crowd of 124,000, Real Madrid made heavy weather of their 2-0 win against a cautious Fiorentina. Real did not open the scoring until twenty minutes from time, when they were fortunate to be awarded a penalty by Leo Horn, the referee from the Netherlands. Fiorentina's Magnini fouled Enrique Mateos, but the latter player had been flagged as offside by a linesman when he began his run towards goal. Di Stefano scored from the penalty, and six minutes later Francisco Gento scored the second goal. The home crowd were delighted to see Real Madrid retain the trophy, which was presented to Miguel Munoz by General Franco, the Fascist dictator of Spain, who was a supporter of the victorious club. Besides retaining the European Cup in 1957, Real Madrid won the Spanish league that year. Di Stefano was voted European Footballer of the Year for 1957, and would win the award again in 1959.

Having become a naturalised Spaniard in 1956, Di Stefano was cleared by FIFA to play for Spain, despite having already appeared for both Argentina and Colombia. Di Stefano is one of only two players to have represented three different countries in international football, the other being Ladislav Kubala. Di Stefano scored a hat trick on his debut for Spain, as they beat the Netherlands 5-1 in January 1957.

During the remainder of that year Di Stefano featured in the qualifiers for the 1958 World Cup, but Spain were eliminated by Scotland.

Real Madrid retained both the Spanish title and the European Cup in 1957-58. Di Stefano was the European Cup's leading scorer this season, with ten goals. Four of these goals came in Real's 8-0 win against Seville, in the first leg of an all-Spanish Quarter Final, and Di Stefano followed this with a hat trick, as Real beat Vasas Budapest 4-0 in the opening match of their Semi Final. Real's opponents in the Final were Milan, with the match played at the Heysel Stadium, in Brussels. This developed into an exciting contest, but only after a nervous, and goalless, first half. Milan twice took the lead, but Real equalised on each occasion, with Di Stefano, who led the fight-back, scoring his team's first goal. During extra time Francisco Gento scored to secure a 3-2 win for Real Madrid. Di Stefano subsequently recalled this match as "the toughest test of all" faced by Real in the early European Cups.

In the 1958-59 European Cup, Di Stefano was sent off in the home leg of Real Madrid's First Round tie against Besiktas. In the Quarter Finals, he scored four times in the 7-1 win at home to Wiener Sport Club. Real required a play-off to beat Atletico Madrid in the Semi Finals, with Di Stefano and Ferenc Puskas scoring in the 2-1 victory. The 1959 Final, played at Stuttgart, brought together Real Madrid and Stade de Reims, in a repeat of the 1956 decider. The match proved to be a disappointing contrast to the excitement of the 1956 contest. Real Madrid won 2-0, with Di Stefano scoring their second goal, but neither team played to their potential.

In 1960 Real Madrid won the European Cup for a fifth successive time, beating Eintracht Frankfurt 7-3 in the Final, which ranks as the greatest match in the history of the competition – indeed it remains among the most brilliant games in any football competition. Prior to this, the Semi Final draw had paired Real Madrid with their bitter rivals, Barcelona. The clash went beyond the confines of football, with a political dimension to the long-established rivalry between the clubs. General Franco's Fascist dictatorship actively associated itself with the success of Real Madrid. By contrast Barcelona represented Catalan nationalism, and the democratic spirit which had made their city a centre of resistance to Franco during the Civil War of 1936-39. Both legs of the Semi Final were excellent contests, and each time Real Madrid won 3-1, with Di Stefano scoring twice in the first leg. These defeats prompted Barcelona to dismiss Helenio Herrera, their manager, but a few weeks later Barcelona won the Spanish title, finishing ahead of Real on goal average.

The Final was played at Hampden Park in Glasgow, before an appreciative crowd of 134,000 people – the highest ever for a European Cup Final – who had paid ticket prices ranging from 5 Shillings (now 25 pence) to 50 shillings (now £2.50). The Real players had been offered a bonus of about £650 per player to win the Final, while Eintracht's players were offered around one tenth of this by a rather frugal management. It all seems very small money compared to the multi-million pound Champions League we are accustomed to in the present day. Eintracht Frankfurt made a bright start, and took the lead after eighteen minutes. The goal stung Real into action, particularly Di Stefano, who single-handedly took control of midfield, and directed the team's attacks. After twenty six minutes, Di Stefano met a cross from Canario, on the six yard line towards the far post, and swept the ball, falling as he did so, into the goal, and Real were level. Real took the lead with half an hour played, as Canario's powerful shot was only parried by Loy, the Eintracht goalkeeper, whereupon Di Stefano thrashed the ball into the roof of the net from three yards. On the stroke of half time, Puskas scored to put Real 3-1 ahead. Puskas was eventually to score four goals in the match, while Di Stefano completed a hat track in the second half, as Real and Eintracht rapidly exchanged goals. Di Stefano's third goal came as he led an exchange of passes from the re-start after an Eintracht goal, and drove a shot from twenty yards that sped across the turf, and into the bottom right-hand corner of the net. Five minutes from time Di Stefano, set free by a long-range pass from Vidal, flicked a shot out of the reach of Loy, only for the ball to thud against a post. Di Stefano therefore missed out on equalling Puskas' haul of four goals in the Final.

As the match ended the enormous crowd – most of them native Scots – rose to acclaim the efforts of Real Madrid and Eintracht Frankfurt with a standing ovation. Those lucky enough to be present knew they had witnessed a game almost without equal. The crowd's appreciation continued for a quarter of an hour, as Zarraga, the Real captain, collected the trophy, following which the players received their medals, and Real ran a lap of honour. Real Madrid had won the European Cup for a fifth successive time, with a golden performance that immortalised the exploits of a team that ranks among the greatest in the history of football. The spectacular football of Real Madrid also gave a great boost to the standing of the European Cup, helping to secure the prominence the competition has always deserved.

In 2005, as the European Cup / Champions League reached its half-century, Di Stefano was interviewed for *Champions: The Official Magazine of the UEFA Champions League*, and drew the following interesting comparison between the competition he had played in, and the modern equivalent: "It was a real Champions Cup. Every team in the competition had won their league in their own country. Not like now. Today it's all about business, that's the way the club want it. For sure it is still a great competition, with a lot of crack players, but it is definitely a business. It all started in the 1950s, with players' pictures and chocolate bars, and today football is a real industry. Then it was another world. There was no advertising, no sponsors' names on jerseys, no TV rights. We used to play a huge amount of friendlies all over the world just to make some money. We travelled across Europe and South America and then the provincial teams came to Madrid to play against us, also to make some money. I used to complain that I had signed a contract to play football not to run all over the world". Di Stefano also recalled that when he arrived at Real Madrid, Bernabeu discouraged the club's players from owning cars, wishing to avoid an ostentatious image. Di Stefano and his wife Sara, along with their three children, found the cost of taxi journeys around Madrid expensive. Di Stefano was eventually given permission by the chairman to buy a small car, in response to a diplomatic request following the 1956 European Cup victory.

A few weeks after their 1960 European Cup Final, Real Madrid moved beyond the confines of Europe to assert their place in the global game, by winning the inaugural World Club Championship, with a victory against Penarol. After a goalless draw in Uruguay, Real won 5-1 in the return leg, with Di Stefano among the goalscorers. Real Madrid won the Spanish league in 1960-61, twelve points clear of runners-up Atletico Madrid, this being their first national title since 1958, but were eliminated by Barcelona in the First Round of the European Cup. The following season saw Real win the league and cup double. Real had been beaten Finalists in the Spanish Cup in 1958, 1960, and 1961, but in 1962 they defeated Sevilla 2-1 to take the Cup. Real also reached the 1962 European Cup Final, but lost 5-3 to Benfica in a pulsating match, despite Puskas scoring a hat trick – while Di Stefano failed to score in a European Cup Final appearance for the first time.

During 1961 Spain qualified for the following year's World Cup finals, with Di Stefano scoring in three of their four qualifying matches. Di Stefano travelled to Chile for the 1962 finals, but did not play in the tournament, due to the combination of a pulled muscle and strained relations with Helenio Herrera, who was Spain's manager. This proved to be an anti-climatic end to Di Stefano's chequered international career. He had scored 23 goals in 31 matches for Spain between 1957 and 1961, thereby taking his international totals to 29 goals in 40 games. Despite being one of the greatest players in the history of the game, Di Stefano never graced the World Cup finals. Prior to missing out with Spain in both 1958 and 1962, two possible opportunities had failed to materialise. When Di Stefano was an international for Argentina they declined to enter the 1950 competition, and by the start of the 1954 qualifiers he had switched his allegiance to Colombia, who were excluded by FIFA. Di Stefano was also unlucky with the European Nations' Cup. Spain's progress in the inaugural 1960 competition was ended by a withdrawal forced by Franco's government, in order to avoid playing the Soviet Union in the Quarter Finals. Spain, as host nation, were ironically to beat the Soviet Union in the 1964 Final, following the end of Di Stefano's career with the national team. There was, however, an alternative recognition of Di Stefano's standing with his selection for the FIFA World XI team that played against England at Wembley in 1963, to mark the centenary of the Football Association. England won 2-1, with Jimmy Greaves scoring the winner in the final minute, shortly after Denis Law had equalised an earlier goal by England's Terry Paine.

Back in Spanish domestic football, Di Stefano helped Real Madrid win the league in both 1963 – with a repeat of the twelve point margin on second-paced Atletico Madrid from a couple of years earlier – and 1964. Real also reached the European Cup Final in 1964, but lost 3-1 to Internazionale, who were managed by Helenio Herrera. During the Summer of 1964 Di Stefano moved from Real Madrid to Espanol, following a rift with Santiago Bernabeu. It was the end of a remarkable era. During the eleven seasons that Di Stefano played for them, Real Madrid had won the Spanish League eight times, the European Cup five times, and the Spanish cup once. Real had also been runners-up in the European Cup twice, while Di Stefano accumulated a total of 49 goals in the competition between 1955 and

1964. Di Stefano spent a couple of years at Espanol, before injury forced his retirement in 1966, at the age of 40.

Following the end of his playing days, Di Stefano enjoyed success as a coach, in both Spain and Argentina. He won the Argentinian title with Boca Juniors in 1969, and River Plate in 1981. In between, Di Stefano had a couple of spells as manager of Valencia, leading them to the Spanish title in 1971, and the European Cup-Winners' Cup trophy in 1980. Across the border, in Portugal, Di Stefano coached Sporting Lisbon during the 1974-75 season. Di Stefano returned to Real Madrid as manager in 1982, and remained in post until 1984. In 1983 Real reached the European Cup-Winners' Cup Final, but lost 2-1 to Aberdeen, who were managed by Alex Ferguson – who had coincidentally been part of the crowd in his native Glasgow at the 1960 European Cup Final. Di Stefano subsequently acted as caretaker manager for Real Madrid, during the 1990-91 season. Elimination from the European Cup, by Spartak Moscow, led to the end of Di Stefano's second spell in charge at Real. That proved to be his final coaching role, but Di Stefano has remained a father figure at Real Madrid. He was appointed Honorary President of the club in November 2000, and has chaired an association of former Real players, which meets regularly. When Real Madrid beat Bayer Leverkusen in the 2002 Champions League Final, at Hampden Park, Di Stefano led a reunion of players who won the 1960 European Cup Final at the same venue. On December 24 2005 Di Stefano, who was now aged 79, suffered a heart attack, and was admitted to hospital in Valencia. Following a heart by-pass operation four days later, Di Stefano made a good recovery. His convalescence was boosted by Real Madrid's decision to name their reserve team ground the Alfredo Di Stefano Stadium. The occasion was marked by a friendly match on May 9 2006, with Real Madrid beating Stade De Reims 6-1, in a repeat of the first European Cup Final, in which Di Stefano had starred fifty years earlier.

In 2000 Di Stefano surveyed his life and career, with the publication of an autobiography, *Gracias Vieja!* (the title is Spanish for "Thanks mum"). Di Stefano has remained a great enthusiast for football, and his personal heritage. During the 2005 interview with *Champions* magazine, Di Stefano explained: "I am mostly Italian, but I have an Irish maternal grandmother and a French grandfather on my father's side. The Irish side means there is something from the British Isles in me. I am still very grateful for what England have done, and are still doing, for football. Thanks to football and the English who invented it, thousands of people live well today – players, clubs, journalists, managers, agents, coaches, a whole community". Besides the absence of any appearance in the World Cup finals, Di Stefano's long-term reputation has been slightly undermined by the relative lack of film of his performances, compared to that of other great players of recent decades – although the BBC coverage of the 1960 European Cup Final is a brilliant document of Di Stefano's talents. Di Stefano was awarded a Super Ballon d'Or in 1989 as Europe's greatest ever player. UEFA's dual poll in 2004 aimed at finding Europe's greatest footballers saw Di Stefano placed fifth by the players and coaches, and sixth by the supporters, both of which were lower rankings than might have been expected. For many players, Di Stefano was the greatest of all time, with George Best, Johan Cruyff, and Diego Maradona each lauding him as their personal hero. In the words of George Best: "Di Stefano was the best footballer ever. He had everything. I used to pretend to be him as a kid".

2 Pele: Planet Football

Pele, possibly the greatest player in the history of football, was born on October 23 1940. During a career lasting more than twenty years, Pele made vital contributions as Brazil won the World Cup three times, and also played a major role in the success of his two clubs, Santos and New York Cosmos. Pele was a prolific goalscorer, a player of incredible skill and imagination, who harnessed these individual qualities to the needs of the teams he was a member of, while always displaying great sportsmanship.

The man who was to become known throughout the world by the nickname Pele was given the full name Edson Arantes do Nascimento at his birth, which took place at Tres Coracoes, in the Brazilian state of Minas Gerais. Pele was born into a poor family, but found a way out of poverty through football, being inspired by his father Dondinho, a professional footballer who struggled to earn the money that his ability merited. Having shown prodigious potential, Pele was signed by Santos, a club based in the city of that name, within the state of Sao Paulo. In 1956, at the age of only fifteen. Pele scored the first goal of his professional career on his debut, as Santos beat Corinthians of Santo Andre (as opposed to the better known Corinthians club, based at Sao Paulo) 7-1. In the following year he gained a place in Brazil's national team, scoring in his debut, which was a 2-1 defeat against Argentina on July 7. Three days later Brazil beat Argentina 2-0, with Pele again among the goalscorers. These two matches comprised the 1957 edition of the Roca Cup, a contest between Argentina and Brazil played at intervals between 1914 and 1976.

As a seventeen year-old Pele helped Brazil win the 1958 World Cup, scoring six goals in his four appearances in the finals. After missing Brazil's first two matches, Pele played in a 2-0 win against the Soviet Union. In the Quarter Finals, Pele scored the only goal of a match against Wales, following which a hat trick helped Brazil beat France 5-2 in the Semi Finals. Pele then scored two goals in the 5-2 win against Sweden, the host nation, in the Final. In 1959 Pele was the leading scorer in the Copa America, with eight goals in six matches, but Brazil finished as runners-up to the hosts Argentina. Surprisingly this was the sole occasion on which Pele played in the competition.

Brazil successfully defended the World Cup at the 1962 finals, staged in Chile, but Pele's role was limited. He scored a brilliant solo goal in the 2-0 win against Mexico, but tore a thigh muscle –

unleashing a long-range shot which hit a post – in the goalless draw with Czechoslovakia in the next match. Pele was unable to take any further part in the tournament, while Garrincha emerged as Brazil's star player. Brazil met Czechoslovakia again in the Final, winning 3-1. In 2007 Pele was retrospectively awarded a 1962 World Cup winners' medal, as FIFA made awards to players who had been part of winning squads but had not previously been awarded the relevant medal.

Pele helped Santos become Brazil's leading club side during the 1960s, as they won various competitions in the fragmented domestic game. A cup competition that brought together the leading teams from the regional leagues served as an effective national championship, and Santos won the trophy each year from 1961 to 1965. Santos went on to win the Copa Libertadores in 1962, defeating Penarol in the Final. This in turn led to participation in the World Club Championship later that year. In the first leg, Santos beat Benfica 3-2, at the Maracana, in Rio de Janeiro, with Pele scoring twice. Santos thrashed Benfica 5-2 in the return match, over in Lisbon, with Pele scoring a hat track – he later wrote "the match was the best game of my career". Santos also completed a treble success, as champions of Brazil, South America, and the world in 1963. After beating Boca Juniors in the Libertadores Final, Santos met Milan for the world title. Santos lost 4-2 at the San Siro, won by the same score at home, and took the play-off, in Rio, with a single goal victory. Pele scored twice in the first leg against Milan, but missed the remaining two matches due to an injury.

Brazil took an ageing team to England for the 1966 World Cup finals. They started with a 2-0 win against Bulgaria, in which Pele scored, but persistent physical challenges by the opposition left him with an injury. This caused Pele to miss the next game, in which Brazil were beaten 3-1 by Hungary. Brazil lost by the same scoreline against Portugal, causing their elimination from the tournament, with Pele suffering a brutal double foul by Morais, which left him as a passenger. Understandably aggrieved, Pele threatened not to play in the next World Cup.

Away from the football pitch, Pele had married Rosemeri Cholbi in February 1966. Pele and Rosemeri were to have three children, Kelly Cristina, born in 1967, Edson in 1970, and Jennifer in 1978. The couple separated shortly after the birth of Jennifer, and were soon divorced, as Rosemeri felt the strain of bringing up children while Pele was often away from home. Pele married for a second time in 1994, his new bride being Assiria Lemos Seixas. Two years later, Pele and Assiria became the parents of twins, named Joshua and Celeste. Pele is also the father of two daughters by other women, the children being Sandra Machado and Flavia Kurtz, who were born in 1964 and 1968 respectively.

In 1968 Santos won a new competition, played on a league basis, to become Brazilian champions for a sixth time. During 1968 and 1969 Santos competed in the Recopa Intercontinental, a tournament that brought together the clubs which had won the World Club Championship since its inception in 1960. Santos reached the Final, and beat Internazionale 1-0 in the first leg, at Milan, following which the Italian club declined to fulfil a second leg. Three years on from the 1966 finals, Pele returned to World Cup football. During August 1969 Pele appeared in each of Brazil's qualifying matches in the 1970 competition, scoring six goals as they chalked up six straight wins. In November 1969 Pele scored the one thousandth goal of his career, in a match for Santos. Pele eventually amassed a career total of 1,283 goals in first class football, a total surpassed by only one other player, Arthur Friedenreich, another Brazilian.

Pele reached the peak of his career at the 1970 World Cup finals, staged in Mexico. Brazil began with a 4-1 win against Czechoslovakia, in which Pele scored once. Prior to his goal, Pele came close to a remarkable feat, as he received the ball in the centre circle and, seeing Ivo Victor, the Czech goalkeeper, standing well of his goal-line, lofted the ball from fifty yards out towards goal. Victor scrambled back, with little chance of reaching the ball, but Pele's brilliance was not rewarded, with the shot travelling just wide. In the next match, Brazil beat England 1-0, but Gordon Banks denied a headed effort from Pele with an amazing save. The game was a great contest, symbolised by an embrace between Pele and Bobby Moore after the final whistle. Pele scored twice in a 3-2 victory against Romania. A 4-2 win against Peru in the Quarter Finals was followed by a 3-1 defeat of Uruguay in the Semi Finals. Pele did not find the target in either of those matches, but again went close with a memorable effort. In the match with Uruguay, Pele and Ladislao Mazurkiewicz, the opposing goalkeeper, were both chasing the ball, Pele ran to the left of his opponent on the edge of the penalty area, while allowing the ball to run to the right. Pele then changed direction, caught up with the ball, and shot from a narrow angle. The ball rolled across the goalmouth, out of the reach of retreating Uruguayans, but also just wide of the far post.

Pele opened the scoring in the Final, with a header, as Brazil beat Italy 4-1 to win the World Cup for the third time in four competitions. This was Pele's twelfth goal in the World Cup finals, twelve years after his arrival on this stage, in Sweden. Four minutes from the end of the 1970 Final, Brazil climaxed their display with an immaculate goal. Tostao intercepted the ball near the Brazilian penalty area, and fed Wilson Piazza, who started a quick interchange of passes which saw the ball move to Clodoaldo, Pele, Gerson, and back to Clodoaldo, who then weaved past four Italians. Clodoaldo then stroked the ball to Rivelino, who in turn sent a long pass down the left wing to Jairzinho. The latter moved inside to lay the ball off to Pele, who pushed it into the path of Carlos Alberto, and he met the ball just inside the penalty area, with a thundering shot past Enrico Albertosi, the Italian goalkeeper.

In 2006 Carlos Alberto was given a trophy by FIFA, who had decided this was the most beautiful goal ever scored in the World Cup. In the same year, Pele explained (in his autobiography) that Brazil tried several times in the match to take advantage of "the avenue", this being space freed on their right wing when Giacinto Facchetti, the Italian left back, followed as Jairzinho moved away from his normal position on the right wing. When Pele received the ball from Jairzinho, who was being tracked by Facchetti, "since I knew Carlos Alberto would be coming in on his own, I passed to him. We had practised the move, and it worked perfectly, Carlos Alberto driving the ball past Albertosi like a thunderbolt". Although Pele does not mention it, film of the goal shows Tostao gesturing to Pele that he could pass to Carlos Alberto. Pele recalled that he and Carlos Alberto established a friendship playing together at Santos: "We had a synchronicity, and that was most delightfully demonstrated in that final World Cup goal".

Pele retired from international football in 1971, having scored a national record of 77 goals in 92 appearances for Brazil. He remained a first choice player for Santos until he left the club in 1974 – sixteen years after his arrival. Lured to the USA by the excitement of the new North American Soccer League, Pele ended his career with New York Cosmos, playing for them from 1975 to 1977. New York Cosmos won the NASL in 1977, at which point Pele retired. A farewell match was staged between New York Cosmos and Santos, in which Pele played one half for each team, scoring for Cosmos, who won 2-1. The 75,000 crowd included Andy Warhol, who remarked "Pele is one of the few who contradicted my theory: instead of fifteen minutes of fame he will have fifteen centuries".

Since ending his playing days, Pele has continued enthusiastic involvement with football, and remained an influential figure. The description of football as "the beautiful game" is a phrase coined by Pele, featuring in an autobiography *My Life and the Beautiful Game*, published in 1977. Four years later, Pele featured alongside various footballers, including Bobby Moore, plus actors, in the football fantasy film *Escape to Victory*. Pele never played at Wembley, but was guest of honour for the Football League Centenary match, staged at the stadium, during 1987. Twenty years later, in 2007, Pele was also guest of honour at a match between Sheffield FC, a non-league team, and Internazionale, which celebrated the 150th anniversary of the formation of Sheffield, recognised by FIFA as the oldest football club in the world. The game was staged at Brammall Lane, home of Sheffield United, with Internazionale winning 5-2. In between these events, Pele received an honorary British knighthood, presented to him by Elizabeth II in 1997. Having been appointed a United Nations ambassador for ecology and the environment in 1992, Pele took on the role of Minister for Sport in the Brazilian government, serving in this post from 1995 to 1998, and overseeing a law that countered football corruption. Commercial ventures have included advertising campaigns for Mastercard and Viagra, the latter combined with Pele drawing attention to the issues surrounding erectile dysfunction. Amidst some controversy, Pele and Diego Maradona were jointly winners of the FIFA Player of the Century award in 2000. Maradona won an Internet vote of supporters, while Pele was selected by FIFA members. Twenty nine years after the publication of *My Life and the Beautiful Game*, there followed *Pele: The Autobiography*, which appeared in 2006, a year in which Pele and Claudia Schiffer paraded the trophy at the World Cup opening ceremony, in Munich. In the Preface to his new book, Pele wrote of his passion for football, and the way in which the game had made him a happy man. The Preface had a sub-title, with a phrase reflecting the unity of a game in which Pele has given so much to people around the world: "Planet Football".

3 Eusebio: The Black Pearl

Eusebio, one of the greatest stars in European football, and arguably Portugal's finest ever footballer, was ironically born in Africa. To be precise he was born at Lourenco Marques in the colony of Portuguese East Africa – now Maputo in Mozambique – on January 25 1942. His full name is Eusebio da Silva Ferreira, but he has always simply been Eusebio to the footballing world. Eusebio, who gained the nickname "the Black Pearl", was a prolific goalscorer, with a career record of 727 goals in 715 games. His ability as a striker combined acceleration, and great dribbling, with a powerful right foot shot. Besides being the star of the Benfica team which reached several European Cup Finals in the 1960s, Eusebio also shone for the Portuguese national team.

During retirement, Eusebio recalled his early years as follows: "I went to school but I was never a good student. In my family we were eight siblings, but I was the only one who spent all my time running after the ball so I didn't go to school for long. I was only there until fourth class. I played football in my neighbourhood barefoot. Then I went to play officially for local club Sporting, but I was in fact a fan of Deportivo. I went to Deportivo three times hoping to train there and three times they turned me down". Eusebio first appeared for the Sporting Club of Lourenco Marques, at the age of sixteen, in 1958. The club acted as a nursery for Sporting Lisbon, and it was expected that Eusebio would move to the latter club, but on arriving in Portugal he was quickly acquired by Benfica. After a legal dispute with Sporting Lisbon that stretched over several months, Eusebio made his debut for Benfica, and helped them to win the Portuguese championship of 1960-61, but did not participate in their victorious European Cup campaign that season. This was the first of eleven championships won by Benfica over the fifteen seasons in which Eusebio featured in their team. Incidentally, Sporting Lisbon were to win the title in each of the other four seasons that Eusebio played for their rivals.

In September 1961 Benfica participated in the second instalment of the World Club Championship. They beat Penarol 1-0 in Lisbon, but were thrashed 5-0 in the return match. The title was contested on the two-legged, home and away, basis used in the European Cup but, during the early years, instead of aggregate score being used, the winners were decided on the number of matches won. The regulations stipulated that if each team won a single match, or if both matches were drawn, a play-off would take place, within a few days of the second leg, and on the continent of the team who had played at home in that leg. Benfica hurriedly flew Eusebio out to Uruguay to play in the decider, and he scored an excellent goal, but Penarol achieved a 2-1 victory. At least justice was done, given the margin of the Uruguayans' win in the second leg.

Eusebio's international reputation grew further in the following month, as he scored on his debut for Portugal, at the age of 19, but the team experienced a surprise 4-2 defeat against Luxembourg in a World Cup qualifier. Eusebio also played for Portugal when they lost 2-0 against England at Wembley later in the same month, a result which put England through to the World Cup finals. Benfica's progress in the 1961-62 European Cup led to a Semi Final meeting with Tottenham Hotspur, who had won the English League and FA Cup double the previous season. Tottenham were strengthened by the inclusion of Jimmy Greaves, who had recently returned to England after a difficult spell with Milan. Spurs paid Milan £99,999 for Greaves, breaking the British transfer record, but avoiding putting the player under excessive pressure with a six figure price. Benfica won a thrilling tie 4-3 on aggregate. Benfica retained the European Cup, with an amazing 5-3 win against Real Madrid in the Final, at Amsterdam's Olympic Stadium. Real took a two goal lead, before Benfica pulled the score back at 2-2, and Real in turn went 3-2 ahead. Benfica equalised again five minutes into the second half. Although Ferenc Puskas had scored a hat trick for Real Madrid in first half, the decisive contribution was to come from Eusebio midway through the second half. With twenty five minutes remaining Eusebio received the ball on the right wing, twenty yards inside the Benfica half, and set off on a powerful run, which took him into the Real penalty area, where he was fouled by Pachin. Eusebio scored from the penalty, to put Benfica ahead for the first time. Three minutes later Coluna rolled a free kick to Eusebio, and the latter's shot from twenty five yards deflected off a member of Real's defensive wall, and out of the reach of their goalkeeper, Araquistain. Benfica controlled the play during the remainder of the match to hold on to a 5-3 victory. Real Madrid had been eclipsed by Benfica, and Eusebio, a player who had only turned twenty midway through the season. The changing order was symbolised at the end of the Final, as Di Stefano swapped shirts with Eusebio. Years later, Eusebio would recall this as the proudest moment of his career. During retirement, Eusebio offered the following assessment of his rival: "For me, Di Stefano is the best player in the history of the game, the most complete. I think Pele, more or less of my age, was a great player. Bobby Charlton, a great player, Beckenbauer, Cruyff, Garrincha, Puskas, all those guys were great players, Rivera, Stanley Matthews, but for me the most complete was Don Alfredo Di Stefano".

Benfica won the Portuguese Cup in 1962, but in the Autumn of that year they were beaten in the World Club Championship for the second successive season, losing 3-2 and 5-2 against Santos. Pele scored five times in the tie for the Brazilian club, whereas Eusebio only found the net once. In 1963 Benfica won the Portuguese League, and reached the European Cup Final, which was held in England for the first time. The staging of the match in the home of football unfortunately did not capture the imagination of the English public, and the attendance at Wembley was 45,715 – less than half of the available capacity. The scheduling on a Wednesday afternoon contributed to the low turnout. Eusebio gave Benfica the lead after eighteen minutes, running half the length of the field with the ball, before hitting a shot that went in via the inside of a post. In the second half Jose Altafini scored twice, as Milan recovered to win 2-1 – a result which ended Benfica's hopes of a hat trick of European trophies. Later in 1963, Eusebio played for the World team beaten 2-1 by England, in the match at Wembley celebrating the centenary of the Football Association.

In 1964 Benfica won the Portuguese league and cup double, thrashing Porto 6-2 in the cup Final. During the 1964-65 European Cup, as Benfica won 5-0 against La Chaux-de-Fonds, Eusebio scored a goal he later remembered as the greatest of his career: "I took a pass from Simoes, dribbled past three defenders, lifted the ball past another, and then smashed it into the net before it hit the ground. As I turned away, I heard the keeper shouting 'Eusebio Eusebio' behind me, and I thought maybe he was going to hit me. He just wanted to congratulate me, and say that by the time he had got his hands up to try to save the shot, the ball was already in the back of the net". In the European Cup Quarter Finals, Benfica thrashed Real Madrid 5-1, with Eusebio scoring twice, before the Spaniards won the return leg 2-1 – the Portuguese therefore took the tie 6-3 on aggregate, three years on from the two teams meeting in the 1962 Final. Benfica went on to reach the 1965 European Cup Final, only to lose 1-0 against Internazionale, managed by Helenio Herrera. The Final was played at the San Siro stadium in Milan, which had been chosen as the venue before the participants were known. Benfica protested to UEFA about having to meet Internazionale on the latter's home ground, but without success. Unfortunately the match proved to be one of the most forgettable of all European Cup Finals. This was largely due to it being played on a very wet pitch, amidst pouring rain. The conditions worked against skilful football, but the defensive attitude of Internazionale was equally to blame, and this was a rare big match in which Eusebio was unable to make an impact. In contrast to this European defeat, Benfica took the Portuguese league title for a third successive season in 1965. Eusebio's central role in the club's consistent success was recognised by his winning the European Footballer of the Year title for 1965. Eusebio was presented with the award on the pitch, immediately before Benfica met Manchester United, in the second leg of a European Cup Quarter Final, in March 1966. United, inspired by George Best, won the match 5-1, to take the tie 8-3 on aggregate.

Eusebio reached the pinnacle of his career a few months later, being one of the outstanding players in the 1966 World Cup finals, with Portugal having qualified for the first time. Eusebio had scored seven goals in the qualifiers, including a hat trick in a 5-1 win against Turkey. He then emerged as the leading goalscorer in the finals, with nine goals in six matches. Portugal beat Hungary 3-1 in their first match, and followed this with a 3-0 victory against Bulgaria, with Eusebio among the scorers in the latter match. Portugal completed the group stage with a 3-1 win against Brazil, in which Eusebio scored twice – his second goal courtesy of a powerful shot from a narrow angle. In the Quarter Finals Portugal met North Korea, the rank outsiders, who had produced the surprise of the tournament by eliminating Italy, with a 1-0 victory in the group stage. North Korea rushed into a 3-0 lead against Portugal in the first twenty minutes. The unknowns were suddenly on the verge of the Semi Finals. Eusebio, however, had other ideas, and led a Portuguese revival. By half time the deficit had been reduced to 3-2, with Eusebio having scored both of his team's goals, the latter from a penalty. In the second half Portugal over-ran North Korea, as Eusebio equalised, and then put his team ahead with his second penalty of the match. After Eusebio's four goal burst, a strike by Augusto completed a 5-3 victory for Portugal. Eusebio then suffered the bitter disappointment of his team's 2-1 defeat against England in the Semi Final. Bobby Charlton scored twice for England, before Eusebio replied with a penalty late in the match.

Eusebio memorably broke down in tears after the final whistle, disconsolate at missing out on an appearance in the Final. Portugal subsequently beat the Soviet Union 2-1 in the Third Place Match, with Eusebio again among the scorers. Eusebio's impact in Britain led to a waxwork model of him being installed at the Madame Tussauds museum in London. His growing reputation also led to an autobiography, *My Name is Eusebio*, published in Portugal during 1966, with a British edition the following year.

Internazionale tried to buy Eusebio from Benfica in 1966, but the idea was blocked by Antonio Salazar, the Portuguese dictator, on the grounds that the export of Eusebio would undermine national pride. Benfica failed to win either the Portuguese league or cup that year, but Eusebio was the leading scorer in the league in the 1965-66. Indeed Eusebio emerged as the Portuguese league's leading scorer in seven seasons – 1963-64, 1964-65, 1965-66, 1966-67, 1967-68, 1969-70 and 1972-73. In two of these campaigns, Eusebio was the European leading scorer, with 42 goals in 1967-68 (six of them in the 8-0 win against Varzim which secured the league title for Benfica) and 40 goals in 1972-73. Another measure of Eusebio's prolific goalscoring was his performance in the European Cup. He scored 46 goals in Benfica's European Cup matches, and was leading scorer in the 1967-68 competition (with six goals) and joint leading scorer in 1965-66 (with seven goals).

After the blip in 1966, Benfica soon returned to winning ways, taking the Portuguese title in both 1967 and 1968. Benfica reached the 1968 European Cup Final, but lost 4-1 to Manchester United, after extra time, at Wembley. Having hit the crossbar with a shot from twenty yards in the first half, Eusebio nearly won the match for Benfica in the closing minutes of normal time, but was denied by a brilliant save from Alex Stepney. The striker immediately congratulated the goalkeeper on the quality of the save, a famous example of the great sportsmanship for which Eusebio was revered. When the match ended, Eusebio joined Bobby Charlton in a tearful embrace, with both players overcome by the emotion of the occasion – two years on their meeting in a World Cup Semi Final. During an interview in 2006, Eusebio recalled the match. "In the Final it was 1-1 and I get a big chance to score the winner in the last minute. I am clear on goal – and only Stepney is there. But I was not in good shape – they find a small fracture later in my right knee. So I move the ball to my left. It is a good shot but straight into Stepney's chest. If it had been my other foot, Benfica would have won that European Cup. It hurt me because they score three in extra-time. But football is also about losing. I looked at Denis Law, Bobby Charlton and George Best. They were all great footballers so I congratulated them. Best was the greatest-ever Number 7 and when he died I sent his family a fax in Belfast. I told them what George meant to me. Whenever I went to England I always see the man inside George Best. I knew that George – not the famous person with his troubles on the outside". This is a great quote, but Eusebio's memory was incorrect in one respect, as Denis Law was not at the European Cup Final – he watched the match on television in a hospital, as he was coincidentally being treated for a knee injury.

In the space of seven years, between 1961 and 1968, Eusebio had played in four European Cup Finals and two World Club Championships, besides the 1966 World Cup finals. At the time of the 1968 European Cup Final, Eusebio was aged 26, and the prospect of further such success lay before him. Eusebio was destined to play professional football for a further ten years, and win several trophies in the process, but the heights of his early career were not maintained. Benfica took the Portuguese league and cup double in 1969, the cup in 1970, the league in 1971, and then the league and cup double – for the third time in less than a decade – in 1972, but Eusebio's contribution was hampered by a recurring knee injury. Benfica remained a force in the European Cup, but did not reach any further Finals during Eusebio's playing career – a defeat in the Semi Finals of 1972 against Ajax ended the team's best run.

The Portuguese national team went into rapid decline after the 1966 World Cup, finishing as runners-up to Bulgaria in their 1968 European Championship group, and then bottom of a group won by Romania in the 1970 World Cup qualifiers. This was followed by Portugal finishing as group runners-up in the qualifiers for both the 1972 European Championship and 1974 World Cup, behind Belgium and Bulgaria respectively. Eusebio remained a vital member of Portugal's team through these campaigns, but played his last international match in a 2-2 draw against Bulgaria, in a World Cup qualifier, in October 1973. Euesbio's final goal for Portugal had been scored in 1-1 draw with Northern Ireland, in a World Cup match in March 1973 – played at Coventry, due to troubles in Northern Ireland. Eusebio played 64 times for Portugal between 1961 and 1973, scoring

41 goals, but the 1966 World Cup finals was his only appearance in a major international tournament.

Although 1973 brought the end of Eusebio's international career, he enjoyed a swan song that year. Benfica won the league, finishing eighteen points clear of runners-up Belenenses, with Eusebio being Europe's leading scorer. Eusebio won the Portuguese league with Benfica for an eleventh time in 1975, and then left Portugal for a new career in North America. He had spells with Rhode Island Oceaners (1975), Boston Minutemen (1975), Toronto Metros-Croatia (1976), and Monterrey (1976), and helped Toronto Metros-Croatia win the North American Soccer League title. Eusebio then went back to Portugal, playing for Beira Mar in the 1976-77 season. This was followed by spells in 1977 with both Las Vegas Quicksilver and Uniao de Tomar, in the USA and Portugal respectively. Eusebio ended his playing days with New Jersey Americans in 1978, retiring at the age of 36.

When his playing days ended, Eusebio returned to Portugal. Eusebio has remained involved with Benfica in a variety of roles – a spell as assistant manager included defeat, on penalties, against PSV Eindhoven in the 1988 European Cup Final. A statue of Eusebio now adorns the entrance to the club's Stadium of Light. Eusebio has been a regular visitor to Mozambique, but has not really been a figurehead for the rise of African football, in contrast to Roger Milla's leadership with the great Cameroon teams of the 1980s and 1990s. Eusebio acted as an ambassador for Portuguese football, when the nation staged the European Championship finals in 2004. During that year, when asked to comment upon his legendary status, Eusebio reflected: "It has been said that I am a legend, but I have never considered myself greater than others. I must say that getting to the top is hard, but staying there for a long time is much more difficult. It is still nice to be recognised nowadays, and I love signing autographs for kids, even though they are far too young to have seen me play. Many of them are not even Benfica supporters. Each night before I go to bed, I sign photographs to give to fans the next day. I always put the date on them. I started with 'Eusebio 1961' and now I am up to 'Eusebio 2004'". Two years later, Eusebio launched an anti-racism campaign by FIFPro, an international football union, at an event staged in South Africa, looking ahead to the 2010 World Cup finals there. In December 2011 Eusebio was admitted to hospital, suffering from pneumonia, but fortunately he made a good recovery. The following month Eusebio, who remained a national hero in Portugal, celebrated his seventieth birthday. Public events included Eusebio being photographed with his wife, Flora, daughters, Carla and Sandra, plus grandchildren, Luis Pedro and Maria Carolina – a proud and united family.

.

4 George Best: The Good, the Bad and the Bubbly

George Best was one of the greatest players ever to emerge in the British Isles but, playing for a mediocre Northern Ireland team, he never appeared in either the World Cup or European Championship finals. At club level, Best also failed to fulfil his true potential, as his career imploded amidst disciplinary disputes, a drink problem, and the pressure of fame. He made and lost a fortune, later recalling "I spent a lot of money on booze, birds, and fast cars – the rest I just squandered". Alcoholism eventually ended Best's life, after clouding his judgement for many years. Before the long decline, Best was the star of Manchester United team from the mid-1960s to the early 1970s, forming a legendary forward line with Bobby Charlton and Denis Law.

Best was born on May 22 1946, in Belfast. George was the son of Dick Best, employed at the Harland and Wolff shipyard, and his wife Ann, who played hockey for Northern Ireland. Best spent his childhood living on Belfast's Cregagh estate, a working class area where Protestants, including the Best family, and Catholics lived side-by-side, before the perennial political conflict re-surfaced with the explosion of "the troubles" in the late 1960s. In his autobiography *The Good, the Bad and the Bubbly*, Best recalled: "From the time I can first remember, from long before I can remember, all I wanted to do was kick a football. There is a photograph of me aged 14 months with a ball at my feet. Most children can barely walk at that age but there I was, already kicking a football around".

At school George displayed great ability in several sports, but little academic inclination. Football was always his favourite sport, and he excelled playing for the Cregagh Boys Club. Bob Bishop, the local scout for Manchester United (he would later discover both Sammy McIlroy and Norman Whiteside) recommended George to the club, advising Matt Busby that "I have found a genius". Shortly after arriving in Manchester for a trial with the club, a homesick and overawed Best returned to Belfast, before being quickly persuaded to travel back to Manchester. He signed with Manchester United as an apprentice in August 1961, and turned professional in 1963, on his seventeenth birthday. With Busby as a great mentor, Best was soon ready for the big stage, making his debut for Manchester United in a 1-0 win against West Bromwich Albion on September 14 1963, and gaining a regular place in the first team during the second half of the season. In February 1964 Best made his European debut as United beat Sporting Lisbon 4-1 in the first leg of a European Cup-Winners' Cup Quarter Final. Best also played in the return, but a 5-0 defeat ended United's run. Best also starred for the United team that won the 1964 FA Youth Cup, beating Swindon Town 5-2 on aggregate in the Final in April.

The talented youngster was rapidly selected to play for Northern Ireland, making his debut in a 3-2 win against Wales in April 1964. In November 1964 Best scored his first goal for Northern Ireland, but they were beaten 2-1 by Switzerland in this 1966 World Cup qualifier. Northern Ireland would eventually finish as runners-up to Switzerland in their group, a point adrift. Best was part of the team that were held to a 1-1 draw away to Albania in their final match, when a victory would have put Northern Ireland into a play-off with the Swiss.

Manchester United won the League in 1965, this being the club's first championship title since the "Busby Babes" had won eight years earlier. Best played in 41 of the 42 matches in the League campaign, and scored 10 goals. United reached the Semi Finals of the Fairs Cup that season, but lost to Ferencvaros, in a play-off – Best appeared in all eleven matches of United's campaign. Manchester United's run in the European Cup of 1965-66 brought Best to international prominence. In a Quarter Final tie that has become justly celebrated, Manchester United met Benfica. After a narrow 3-2 win at Old Trafford, United appeared likely to face a tough test at the Stadium of Light, where Benfica's European Cup record was won seventeen, drew one, and lost none. United produced a brilliant display of attacking football, building up a three goal lead in the first quarter of an hour, and going on to win 5-1 on the night – thereby completing an 8-3 aggregate victory. United were inspired by Best who scored twice, the latter goal being a brilliant solo effort. After the match, the Portuguese fans saluted Best, who they nicknamed "El Beatle" – seeing him as a superstar on a par with the Beatles. After spending the day following the match in Lisbon, United flew home to Manchester with Best wearing an enormous sombrero. United were subsequently defeated by Partizan Belgrade in the Semi Finals. Best played in the first leg, but was struggling with a knee injury, which caused him to miss the remainder of the season.

Manchester United were English champions again in 1967, with Best an ever-present member of the team in the League, and scoring ten goals, one of them in the 6-1 win against West Ham United that clinched the title. The following year United became the first English club to win the European Cup, beating Benfica 4-1, after extra time, in the Final at Wembley. Despite the attentions of tough-tackling Benfica defenders, Best put in a great display. At the start of extra time, as a clearance from United's goalkeeper, Alex Stepney, was headed on by Brian Kidd, Best took advantage of hesitancy in Benfica's defence to score a brilliant goal, eluding a defender and then taking the ball around the advancing goalkeeper, Henrique, before putting it into an empty net. Best's contribution to United's triumph led to his winning the European Footballer of the Year award for 1968, at the age of 22. Best also won the domestic footballer of the year titles in both England and Northern Ireland during 1968.

In the Autumn of 1968 United were defeated in the World Club Championship by Estudiantes de La Plata, from Argentina. Estudiantes won their home leg 1-0, and then drew 1-1 at Old Trafford, with Best being sent off for fighting in the latter match. United reached the European Cup Semi Finals in 1969, but were beaten by Milan. Over the next few years United's domestic form slipped, and they failed to regain the League title. United's consequent failure to return to the European Cup immediately after the 1968-69 season was particularly disappointing for Best, who subsequently lamented that the club rested upon its laurels after winning the trophy, rather than pressing for further success: "With a bit of foresight, 1968 could have been the start of three or four years domination of Europe. For me, personally, the later years when we were out of Europe were depressing. I hear people say the League championship is the most important thing to win. It was only important to me because it meant we were in the European Cup the following year. There was so much atmosphere at those games. For one thing they were usually night matches, which I loved. They were one-offs, and I missed them terribly. After we were out of Europe, there was just an empty feeling".

Best increasingly filled the emptiness with drink and womanising. Best's fame had rapidly spread beyond football, and he enjoyed a superstar lifestyle. During the early years of his playing career, Best had developed business interests, owning boutiques and night clubs. At the end of the 1960s, Best moved into a famous luxury house, full of state of the art gadgets. He also began a romance with Eva Haraldsted, a young Danish woman, that rapidly led to an engagement, announced in 1969, which George soon broke off. This was the first in a series of high-profile romances for George. The excitement of his champagne lifestyle compensated Best for disappointments on the football pitch, but drink and other distractions also unhinged his career. Much of United's decline could be attributed to the failure to effectively replace Matt Busby, following his retirement as manager. Wilf McGuiness and Frank O'Farrell rapidly came and went, either side of a short return from retirement by Busby. Matt Busby's calm authority had been a steadying influence on Best, whose waywardness suddenly increased. Willie Morgan, who played alongside Best at United, later recalled: "George thought he was the James Bond of soccer. He had everything he wanted, money, girls, and tremendous publicity. He lived from day to day and right up until the end he got away with it. When he missed training or ran away people made excuses for him. He didn't even have to bother to make them himself. He just didn't care".

The start of the 1970s brought intermittent glory for Best, and the beginning of the end of his career. In February 1970 he scored six goals as Northampton Town were beaten 8-2 in the FA Cup. United reached the FA Cup Semi Final that year, only to be beaten by Leeds United, losing 1-0 in a second replay after two goalless draws. This was the fourth time in the space of seven seasons that United had been beaten at this stage, and Best never got to play in an FA Cup Final. In 1971 Best scored an international hat trick, as Northern Ireland were beaten 5-0 in a European Championship qualifier – these proved to be Best's last ever goals for his country. After his injury in 1966 Best rarely missed matches for United over the next six years, and was the club's leading scorer in the League in five successive seasons between 1967-68 (when he netted 28 times) and 1971-72. This consistency came to an abrupt halt, as Best's frustration led to disputes with the club, and his announcement in May 1972 that he was retiring from football – he was aged just 25 at the time. Best changed his mind within a few days, but a real withdrawal from the game followed in November 1972, and lasted nearly a year, as he did not return to the United team until October 1973. Clashes with Tommy Docherty, the new United manager, led to Best's final break with the club at the start of 1974. Best had played 470 matches for United, in a period of just over ten years, scoring 179 goals. He had won the European Cup with the club, and the League Championship twice, but felt that the club had failed to fulfil its potential.

In July 1974 Best made a return of sorts to football, with a few appearances for non-league Dunstable Town. At the end of 1975 he had short spells with Stockport County, a Fourth Division club, and Cork Celtic, in the Republic of Ireland. The following year saw Best play the first of a series of seasons in the USA, featuring for Los Angeles Aztecs in the new North American Soccer League. Best returned to something approaching football normality during the English season of 1976-77, as a regular member of the Fulham team, in which he formed a great duo with Rodney Marsh.

The semi-resurrection of Best's career brought a short recall to the Northern Ireland team – his return in 1976 coming three years after his preceding match for his country. Best bowed out of international football in the 1978 World Cup qualifiers, having played 37 matches for Northern Ireland between 1964 and 1977, scoring 9 goals. Best and goalkeeper Pat Jennings had made their international debuts in the same match, but Jennings was to go on to appear 119 times for Northern Ireland, before retiring at the 1986 World Cup finals. When Best died, Jennings paid the following tribute to his former team-mate: "What people don't realise is that Best was a box-to-box player, not just a winger or the great entertainer. That's what set him apart from other greats, his work-rate and willingness to chase back, to dig in when it was needed. He would always come back when I had the ball and say 'Give it to me', and then go and beat the defenders who were trying to kick him. It was his way of making them feel smaller".

Best rapidly settled in the USA, where the low profile of soccer allowed him relative anonymity, in contrast to the pressures he faced in Britain. Best set up home with Angela MacDonald James, an American woman, whom he married in 1978, and the couple had a son, named Callum. Best continued to play for Los Angeles Aztecs in both 1977 and 1978, before moving on to Fort Lauderdale Strikers, being at the latter club in 1978 and 1979. Then Best leapt to Scotland, playing for Hibernian in the 1978-79 season. A final spell in the USA with San Jose Earthquakes followed in 1980 and 1981. In the latter year, Northern Ireland qualified for the 1982 World Cup finals, and there was speculation that Best might appear in the tournament. This was dispelled as Billy Bingham, the national team manager, remarked that Best's performances were "more like a cornflake than an earthquake". During 1981 Best, now aged 35, also expressed a wish to return to Manchester United and Ron Atkinson, the club's new manager, said he would welcome Best joining United for training, but nothing came of this. Bryan Robson joked that Atkinson's motive was to secure Best as a drinking partner. In the absence of a swansong at Old Trafford, Best's final matches in the English domestic game were played with Bournemouth in 1983, following which he moved to Australia, appearing for Brisbane Lions. Best's last ever first class match was played for Tobermore United in February 1984, as they lost 7-0 against Ballymena United in the Irish Cup – this being his only appearance in Northern Ireland's domestic football. What had passed for a football career during a decade of decline for Best was finally over.

Besides love of the game, financial pressures contributed to Best's long succession of comebacks. Best's massive earnings were offset by the effects of limited business sense, and an extravagant lifestyle, which led to him being officially declared bankrupt in November 1982. Best's life rapidly sank to a new low, as at the end of 1984 he was convicted for drink-driving, and imprisoned for three months. In 1986 Best's marriage to Angela ended in divorce. Following this, Best enjoyed a relationship with Mary Shatila for several years, and benefited from the stability that this mature woman brought to his life. Through all the ups and downs, Best remained an influence in football circles. During the latter stages of his playing career, Best had started to feature as a television football pundit, and this was to continue through much of his retirement. Best was also in demand as an after dinner speaker, and appeared in theatres as a double act with Rodney Marsh.

The developing story of Best's amazing life, often the subject of tabloid sensationalism, fascinated the public, and he supplemented his earnings with a series of books. During his playing career, Best had produced three autobiographies, *Best of Both Worlds* (1968), *On the Ball* (1970), and *Where Do I Go From Here?* (1981). These were followed by a brave retrospective of his life in *The Good, the Bad and the Bubbly*, published in 1990, as Best honestly admitted the way in which drink had harmed him. Best published *Blessed: My Autobiography* in 2001, with this being his most candid book. Best was to produce two further books, which brought together recollections of his career, *Scoring at Half-Time* (2003) and *Hard Tackles and Dirty Baths: The Inside Story of Football's Golden Era* (2005). Drink remained a problem, most famously when in September 1990 Best was clearly drunk while interviewed by Terry Wogan, on the latter's BBC chat show. Years later, in *Blessed*, Best recalled: "The worst thing was that I thought I'd got away with it, that though I might have been a bit tipsy, I had come across as reasonably coherent. But when I saw the recording the following day, it was obvious that I had been completely out of it. It's awful to see yourself coming across as some mumbling drunk".

The lure of young ladies also continued to be a theme for Best. His relationship with Mary Shatila ended as Best began a romance with Alex Pursey, an English woman who was twenty five years younger than him. George and Alex were married in 1995. For a while Best's relationship with Alex proved beneficial, as they settled in the quaint town of Petersfield in Hampshire. Best also began regular work with Sky television as a football pundit in 1998. The long-term effects of alcoholism were now threatening Best, who was given the lifeline of a liver transplant in 2002. Best managed for a short time to give up drink, but was soon back to his old ways, and his drunken behaviour prompted Alex to leave him. At the start of 2004 Best was banned from driving, having been caught drinking and driving. This year also brought Best's second divorce, as his marriage with Alex ended.

In October 2005 Best was admitted to a London hospital with kidney problems, and it was clear that his life was in danger. After several weeks in hospital, and intermittent hope of recovery, George Best died on November 25 2005, aged 59, as a result of multiple organ failure stemming from alcoholism. His funeral was held in Belfast on December 3. As the funeral procession made its way from the Best family home to Stormont, the route was lined with 100,000 mourners. The funeral service at Stormont was broadcast live on television, before a private burial, at which Best's body was interred alongside that of his mother, whose death back in 1978 was partly caused by alcoholism. George's death, after many years of decline, was a tragedy, but the memories of his genius as a footballer, and amazing personality, would always remain. Among the many tributes paid to Best on the day of his death, one of the most thoughtful was the following from Bobby Charlton, who had shared the golden days of the 1960s with Best: "Manchester United's glorious history has been created by people like George Best. Anyone who witnessed what George could do on the pitch wished they could do the same. He made an immense contribution to the game, and enriched the lives of everyone who saw him play. George was on a par, at least, with anyone you can name and, from the conversations I've had with him over the years, I know Pele would tell you the same thing. From a talent and style point of view, I would say Cruyff was probably the nearest thing to him. George was braver, but Cruyff had great organising ability".

The final word on his life should belong to Best. The following sentences, which served as the conclusion to *The Good, the Bad and the Bubbly* in 1990, express a positive theme that Best often reinforced, even in the weeks immediately before his death: "I played the game when it was fun and free and the crowds roared with pleasure, not hate. I scored goals that people still cherish in their memories and tell their children about. If football is an art I was an artist, and I'm proud of that. I won two League championship medals and I took Manchester United to victory in the European Cup. When I was a little boy growing up on the Cregagh estate in Belfast I wanted to be a footballer more than anything else. Years later, Pele called me the greatest footballer in the world. That is the ultimate salute to my life".

5 Johan Cruyff: Dutch Master

Johan Cruyff was the star of the Ajax team that won the European Cup three years in succession during the early 1970s. On a personal level, Cruyff won the European Footballer of the Year award three times, and established himself as the arguably the greatest player in the world, in succession to Pele, who retired from international football in 1971. With both Ajax and the national team of the Netherlands, Cruyff played a leading role in the development of Total Football, an exciting, if short-lived, phenomenon. In a break with traditional categorisation, Cruyff – who wore a number 14 shirt for both club and country – was nominally a centre forward, but enjoyed a roving role, which would also take him out to the wings, or back to a deep-lying position. In this respect, Cruyff emulated his hero, and role model, Alfredo Di Stefano. Besides having great vision, pace, and goalscoring ability, Cruyff introduced a legendary drag back, which often wrong-footed defenders. Cruyff's only fault appeared to be a volatile temperament, which often led him into controversy.

Cruyff was born on April 25 1947, in Amsterdam. At the age of twelve he joined the youth programme at Ajax, with help from his mother, who was employed by the club as a cleaner. Cruyff made rapid progress, and was put into the first team as a seventeen year-old in 1964 by Vic Buckingham, the English manager of Ajax. Buckingham would later describe Cruyff as "God's gift to mankind, in the football sense". Buckingham departed in 1964, being replaced by Rinus Michels, a former centre forward for Ajax who had played five times in the 1950s for a Dutch national team that was midway through a long period in the international wilderness. Football in the Netherlands was played on an amateur basis until 1954, when it became semi-professional. Full professionalism was introduced in 1964. Over the next few years, Michels led Ajax to a series of domestic honours. He imposed strong discipline within the club, earning the nickname "Iron Rinus", but encouraged the players to express themselves on the field. Michels stands as one of the most influential managers in the history of football, being generally regarded as the inventor of "Total Football", an idea that rejuvenated the game. The theory was that static team formations should be replaced with a system where all of the outfield players were capable of inter-changing their roles. It was not totally flexible in practice, but it did produce some brilliant football.

Ajax won the Dutch championship in 1966 (for the first time since 1960), finishing seven points clear of the previous year's champions, Feyenoord. Ajax and Feyenoord were to be fierce rivals over the next few years, as the clubs filled the top two positions in the Dutch league at the end of eight consecutive seasons from 1965-66 to 1972-73. In September 1966 Cruyff made his debut for the national team, and scored a last-minute equaliser in the Netherlands' 2-2 draw with Hungary in a European Championship qualifier. Cruyff's second match for the Netherlands was not a success, as he was sent off in a 2-1 defeat against Czechoslovakia in November 1966. This led to an exclusion from the national team. Following his return in 1967, Cruyff was to be a regular member of the Dutch team for a decade. The 1966 league title was the first of a hat trick for Ajax, as they retained the Dutch championship in 1967 and 1968, with Cruyff emerging as the star of the team. In 1967 Ajax won the league and cup double, beating NAC Breda 2-1 in the Cup Final. Ajax also became serious contenders in the European Cup. In 1966-67 Ajax reached the Quarter Finals, beating Liverpool 7-3 on aggregate on the way, with Cruyff scoring three goals in the tie. Ajax reached the Final in 1969, but lost 4-1 to Milan, with Cruyff not fully fit. In 1970 Ajax won the Dutch league and cup double, for the second time in four seasons, beating PSV Eindhoven 2-0 in the Cup Final.

In 1970-71 the Ajax team fulfilled its potential, by winning the European Cup, beating Panathinaikos in the Final, which was played at Wembley, before a crowd of 83,179 – many of whom had made the relatively short journey from the Netherlands. Ajax took the lead after five minutes, as Van Dijk headed in a cross from Keizer, and always looked likely to win. With three minutes remaining Ajax scored again, to complete a 2-0 victory. A fine run by Cruyff set up an opportunity for Arie Haan, whose shot was deflected into the net by Kapsis, for an own goal. Ajax also retained the Dutch Cup in 1971, beating Sparta Rotterdam in a replayed Final. In a personal triumph, Cruyff won the European Footballer of the Year title in 1971, becoming the first Dutchmen to achieve this honour.

Michels left Ajax after the 1971 European Cup victory. He replaced Vic Buckingham (who preceded him at Ajax) as manager of Barcelona, with that club offering him more money than he could earn at Ajax. The new manager at Ajax was Stefan Kovacs, a Romanian who led the club to even greater heights in the 1971-72 season, winning the European Cup plus the Dutch league and cup. This was

41

the third successive season in which Ajax won the cup, with Den Haag being beaten 3-2 in the Final. Cruyff was the top scorer in the Dutch championship, with 25 goals, and the joint leading scorer in the European Cup with five goals. Internazionale were beaten 2-0 in the European Cup Final, staged at Rotterdam – on the ground of Feyenoord, Ajax's greatest rivals. Cruyff excelled, and scored both goals.

In September 1972 Ajax won the World Club Championship, beating Independiente 4-1 on aggregate, with Cruyff scoring once. This was followed by a 6-3 aggregate victory over Rangers in the inaugural European Super Cup, in January 1973 – Cruyff netted in both legs. At the end of the 1972-73 season, Ajax retained the Dutch title, and also won the European Cup, beating Juventus 1-0 in the Final, played in Belgrade. Johnny Rep scored the goal after four minutes. Ajax played some brilliant football, sending the Juventus players round in circles, with Cruyff being the orchestrator, but failed to take the further goalscoring chances that they created. Ajax had deservedly won the European Cup for the third successive season, with this being the best run of victories since that achieved by Real Madrid in the opening five seasons of the competition. Cruyff's fame had now reached such heights that a documentary film, *Number 14 – Johan Cruyff*, was a major success in cinemas across the Netherlands during the Spring of 1973.

In the Summer of 1973 Cruyff moved from Ajax to Barcelona, for a world record fee of £922,000 – following in the footsteps of Michels. The prospect of massive earnings persuaded Cruyff to move, with Michels commenting that "football is a business, and business is business". In Cruyff's first season with the club, Barcelona won the Spanish league of 1973-74 – their first league title since 1960. The birth of Jordi Cruyff, the son of Johan and his wife Danny, at Amsterdam in February 1974, also helped build what was to become an enduring bond between the player and his new club. The birth was induced, to enable Johan to share the event with his wife, before rushing back to Spain for a vital league fixture, in which he helped Barcelona thrash Real Madrid 5-0. The name Jordi was chosen simply because Danny liked it, but it also happened to be the name of the patron saint of Catalonia. Use of the name for Spanish children had actually been prohibited by General Franco's government, but with Jordi having been born in the Netherlands, the Spanish dictatorship was unable to prevent its use in this case. Johan and Jordi thereby became unintentional symbols of Catalan defiance of Madrid.

At international level Cruyff was the star of an emerging Netherlands team. They failed to reach the finals of either the 1970 World Cup or the European Championships of 1968 and 1972, but showed promise. Cruyff scored five goals in the 1972 European Championship qualifiers, including a hat trick in the 8-0 win against Luxembourg. Following this, Ajax players provided the backbone of the national team which qualified for the 1974 World Cup – their first appearance in the finals since 1938. Cruyff scored eight goals in the qualifiers, as the Netherlands edged into the finals ahead of Belgium on goal difference. Rinus Michels was appointed manager of the Dutch team especially for the finals – with Frantisek Fadrhonc, the previous coach, acting as his assistant. The tournament, held in West Germany, was the highlight of Cruyff's international career. A team of Dutch masters, with Cruyff in amazing form, dazzled a series of opponents. Cruyff also showed his individualism, by refusing to wear the team's Adidas shirt during the tournament, as he had a deal with rival company, Puma. In the first round, the Netherlands beat Uruguay 2-0 and Bulgaria 4-1, either side of a goalless draw with Sweden. The Dutch began the second group stage with a 4-0 annihilation of Argentina, in which Cruyff scored twice. For the first of these goals, Cruyff received a chipped pass on the edge of the penalty area, controlling the ball superbly, before waltzing around the advancing goalkeeper, Daniel Carnevali, to score. The Dutch followed this with a 2-0 win against East Germany. Requiring a draw against Brazil to book a place in the Final, the Dutch beat the reigning world champions 2-0. Cruyff set up the first goal, scored by Neeskens, and added the second himself.

In the Final the Netherlands would meet West Germany, who had adapted the ideas of "Total Football" from their neighbours and rivals. The Dutch team's preparation for the match was disrupted by a lurid story in *Bild Zeitung*, a German tabloid newspaper. In the first minute a run by Cruyff through West Germany's defence was curtailed by a foul from Uli Hoeness. A penalty was awarded, from which Johan Neeskens scored. West Germany recovered from this early set back, and equalised with a penalty from Paul Breitner, before Gerd Muller put them ahead a couple of minutes before the interval. As the players left the pitch for half time, Cruyff complained at length to Jack Taylor, the English referee, about the lack of protection he had received from the tough marking of Bertie Vogts, and was booked for his protest. The Dutch dominated the second half, but were unable to score, leaving West Germany as 2-1 winners. The Dutch had been the best team in the tournament, but were left without the World Cup title. Looking back on his career, in an interview in 2004, Cruyff made an interesting point: "Soccer is a sentimental thing because you belong to a club, you belong to their colours. At the same time, reducing the emphasis on winning a little is important. For example, our Dutch team lost one of the most important games in our lives, the 1974 World Cup Final. But that brought us more fame than we could ever have got by winning because everyone wanted us to win and we didn't. Most of the time, losing can make you bigger. Of course we had to win to get into the Final and that meant everybody was satisfied. But the Final you can win or lose because that's football. For weeks nobody was talking about winning or losing, the spectators in every country were saying 'I want to see that football, they play so nice, that is how football should be'. The result, it did not even bother me".

Cruyff won the European Footballer of the Year award for both 1973 and 1974. He also participated in Barcelona's run to the European Cup Semi Finals in 1974-75. Michels was blamed for their defeat against Leeds United in the Semi Finals, and left the club shortly afterwards. Following a brief return to Ajax, Michels had a second spell at Barcelona between 1976 and 1978. After the league success in 1974, Barcelona surprisingly gained only one further trophy during Cruyff's spell with the club, this being the Spanish Cup in 1978. Following on from their great performance in the 1974 World Cup, the Dutch won a tough group in the 1976 European Championship qualifiers, finishing ahead of Poland (who had taken third place in the World Cup) on goal difference, with Italy just a point behind. The Netherlands eliminated Belgium in Quarter Finals, to take a place in the finals of the competition – restricted at that time to four teams – for the first time. Cruyff was part of the Dutch team which lost to Czechoslovakia in the Semi Finals, but was absent from the victory against Yugoslavia, the hosts, by which the Netherlands took third place. In February 1977 Cruyff gave what he later described as his best ever performance, as he inspired a 2-0 victory for the Netherlands against England, at Wembley. That year, however, brought the end of his international career. He made a good contribution to his team's campaign in the World Cup qualifiers, but said he would not play in the following year's finals, due to security fears in Argentina. Cruyff bowed out with a total of 33 goals in his 48 appearances for the Netherlands.

Cruyff's contribution to the 1978 World Cup finals was limited to the role of a studio pundit for ITV, where he worked alongside Brian Clough. Shortly before his death in 2004, Clough voted for Cruyff as the latter took first place in a UEFA poll of players and coaches, aimed at establishing who were Europe's most brilliant footballers. Clough explained his vote as follows: "Johan Cruyff was so talented he made opponents look like chumps for a pastime. He had pace, great dribbling skills, never faded from a game, and dominated matches with his massive ego. On top of that, he was a great captain and orchestrator, who hated giving the ball away". Clough's point about the importance of the player's ego mirrors the view of Cruyff, who has said: "Football is a game you play with your brain. The game consists of different elements: technique, tactics, and stamina. But the main thing is tactics: insight, trust, and daring".

In 1979 Cruyff, having planned to retire at this point, joined the growing exodus of European stars to the North American Soccer League, where he played for Los Angeles Aztecs – who were now coached by Michels – and then Washington Diplomats. Disliking the artificial pitches in the USA, Cruyff returned to Spain in 1981, joining Levante. He soon moved back to his homeland, and Ajax, with whom he won the Dutch league in 1982, followed by the league and cup double in 1983. Cruyff also won the league and cup double in 1984, but as part of a Feyenoord team, as his playing career ended with a short spell at the arch-rivals of Ajax.

Cruyff rapidly moved into management, enjoying successful spells in charge of both Ajax and Barcelona, the two clubs at the centre of his playing career. Besides the winning of trophies, Cruyff's success as a manager was reflected in the continuation of the tactical innovation that had been a vital part of his brilliance as a player. He led Ajax to the European Cup-Winners' Cup in 1987, beating Locomotive Leipzig 1-0 in the Final. Two years later Cruyff won the same trophy with Barcelona, as they beat Sampdoria 2-0 in the Final. In 1991, shortly after Cruyff had recovered from a heart attack, Barcelona appeared in the European Cup-Winners' Cup Final again, but were beaten 2-1 by Manchester United, in Rotterdam. In the following year, Cruyff led Barcelona to win the European Cup for the first time, with Sampdoria being the beaten Finalists – Ronald Koeman, a fellow-Dutchman, scored the only goal with a brilliant strike in extra time.

On the domestic front, Cruyff's Barcelona broke the dominance of Real Madrid, and won the Spanish league in four successive years from 1991 through to 1994. In the last of those years Barcelona also reached the European Cup Final, but were crushed 4-0 by Milan. Thereafter a dip in Barcelona's form threatened Cruyff's position. There were also suggestions within the club that the manager was unduly favouring Jordi – his son having now become part of the squad – and also Jesus Angoy, a player who was married to Johan's daughter, Chantal. Cruyff was dismissed in 1996, being replaced by Bobby Robson, the former England manager. Cruyff was bitter at the way in which his association with the club ended, and avoided a return to football management for several years.

Cruyff found an alternative channel for his talents, through the Johan Cruyff Foundation, formed in 1997, which has successfully run events for children, with a focus on children with a disability, in many countries throughout the world. Cruyff has explained the role of this organisation as follows: "Children have the right to sport and recreation, as stated in the UN Convention on the Rights of the Child. We believe that through sports children build up social skills, learn how to win and lose, how to develop tactics and strategy. As a result children develop self-confidence and a sense of achievement. But mainly, sports can be plain fun!".

In 2004 the Dutch football association asked the advice of Cruyff when appointing a new coach. Cruyff's recommendation influenced the surprise appointment of Marco Van Basten, who had very little previous coaching experience. Thereafter Cruyff acted as an advisor to Van Basten, who led the Dutch team to the finals of the 2006 World Cup and 2008 European Championship. Van Basten moved to become coach of Ajax in 2008, but a planned return for Cruyff as Technical Director did not go ahead, as Cruyff withdrew due to a professional disagreement between the two men. In the following year, Cruyff became manager of the Catalonia national team, on the fringes of international football. His first match in charge saw Catalonia beat Argentina 4-2, at the Nou Camp. During 2010 Cruyff was made an honorary president of Barcelona, but then stripped of this title, amidst an argument about the internal democracy of the club. Another return to the past saw Cruyff appointed as an advisor to the board of directors of Ajax in 2011, following which he became embroiled in a power struggle at the club. In 2012 Cruyff took on another advisory role, at Club Deportivo Guadalajara, in Mexico. Decades after the peak of his playing career, Cruyff continues to build upon his legendary status as one of the greatest figures in the history of football.

6 Kevin Keegan: Mighty Mouse

Kevin Keegan was among the outstanding players of his generation, winning the European Cup with Liverpool, reaching the Final with Hamburg, and twice being voted European Footballer of the Year. He also played 63 times for England, scoring 21 goals. Keegan's playing career has been followed by a variety of managerial roles, including a spell as England coach. All of this sprang from modest beginnings. Keegan lacked either great height (at 5 feet 8 inches) or physical stature, and was not blessed with natural footballing talent, but he more than compensated for this with work-rate, and determination to succeed. It was a combination that led to Keegan being nicknamed "Mighty Mouse" by the fans of Hamburg when he played for that club.

Keegan was born on February 1 1951, at Armthorpe in Yorkshire. After leaving school, he was employed at a brass factory in Doncaster, and played in the works' football team. This led to Keegan being signed in 1968 by Scunthorpe United, who were relegated to the Fourth Division that year. In 1971 Keegan moved to Liverpool, who paid Scunthorpe a fee of £35,000. Keegan gained a regular place in the Liverpool team during the 1971-72 season, helping them to third place in the League, just a point behind the champions, Derby County.

In November 1972 Keegan made his debut for England, appearing in a 1-0 win against Wales, this being a World Cup qualifier. At the end of the 1972-73 season Liverpool won the League, and Keegan scored twice in the 3-2 aggregate win against Borussia Monchengladbach in the UEFA Cup Final. A year later Keegan also netted twice, as Liverpool beat Newcastle United 3-0 in the 1974 FA Cup Final. In between those two finals, Keegan appeared in Liverpool's short campaign in the 1973-74 European Cup, which was ended by a couple of defeats against Red Star Belgrade in the Second Round. In May 1974, shortly after Liverpool's FA Cup final win, Keegan scored his first goal for England, as Wales were beaten 2-0 in a British Championship match.

Bill Shankly, the legendary Liverpool manager who signed Keegan, retired in 1974, and the club, seeking continuity, chose Bob Paisley, his assistant, as successor. It was initially felt by many, including himself, that Paisley would not be able to emulate the achievements of the extrovert Shankly. Paisley was a quiet and modest man, but he had a great deal of experience at Liverpool, and was able to motivate the team to even greater success over the following years. The Summer of 1974 brought a low point for Keegan, as he and Billy Bremner, of Leeds United, were sent off for fighting in the Charity Shield, following which each player received a lengthy suspension. In 1976 Liverpool repeated the dual League and UEFA Cup victory of 1973, beating Brugge 4-3 on aggregate in the Final of the latter competition, with Keegan accounting for two of the goals.

Keegan's Liverpool career climaxed during the 1976-77 season, amidst considerable speculation that he would leave the club, which eventually proved founded, as a £500,000 transfer to Hamburg was agreed. During the latter part of the season a great deal of attention was focussed on the attempt by Liverpool to achieve a treble, by winning the Football League, FA Cup, and European Cup. The League title was duly won, but Liverpool's attempt to complete the domestic double failed, as they were beaten 2-1 by Manchester United in the FA Cup Final. Hopes of the treble had therefore been ended when Liverpool travelled to Rome to meet Borussia Monchengladbach in the European Cup Final, which was played on May 25, just four days after the FA Cup Final. Liverpool sought to lift themselves again, and become the first British club to win the European title since Manchester United had done so nine years earlier. Borussia Monchengladbach, who had been beaten by Liverpool in the UEFA Cup Final four years earlier, were formidable opponents, as they won West Germany's Bundesliga for the third successive year in 1977 – they had also won the UEFA Cup in 1975. Liverpool produced a great display to beat Borussia 3-1. One of the main reasons for Liverpool's control of the match was the performance of Keegan, whose consistently inventive attacking play gave Berti Vogts, his ever-attendant marker, a torrid time. As the players walked into the tunnel at half time, Keegan asked Vogts "Are you going into our dressing room or yours?" In the closing minutes of the second half, Keegan's torment of Vogts culminated with a powerful run into the Borussia area, which caused the German to concede a penalty, by bringing down the Englishman. Phil Neal scored from the penalty, and completed Liverpool's historic victory.

The Liverpool players and club officials held a celebratory banquet at their hotel, and Berti Vogts sportingly dropped in to buy Keegan a drink. Keegan later recalled his feelings after the match: "At the end I just felt flat. It was the end of my Liverpool career, and already it was in the past. The fans had given me a bit of stick about going, but I had tried to be honest. I only half did the lap of honour. Everybody said my battle with Vogts was the key to Liverpool's victory, but frankly I would not put the European Cup Final among my best ten games for Liverpool. The thing I remember most was Bertie coming to sit with me at the reception afterwards. He came along to congratulate us. I said to Jean, my wife, what a gesture that was. I do not think I could have done it". This was the beginning of a lasting friendship between Keegan and Vogts, the latter of whom would later manage Germany and Scotland.

A fortnight before Liverpool won the European Cup, Hamburg had beaten Anderlecht 2-0 in the European Cup-Winners' Cup Final. This led to a meeting between Keegan's old and new clubs at the end of 1977, in the European Super Cup. After a 1-1 draw in West Germany, Keegan's return to Anfield for the second leg was not the homecoming he hoped for, as Liverpool thrashed Hamburg 6-0, with Terry McDermott scoring a hat trick, to become the first British club to take the Super Cup. Liverpool also retained the European Cup that season, beating Brugge 1-0 in the Final, with a goal from Kenny Dalglish, a player whose purchase from Celtic in August 1977 had been funded by the fee received for Keegan.

Keegan initially found it hard to settle at Hamburg, with other players at the club feeling resentful at the arrival of a high-profile outsider, and going as far as refusing to pass the ball to him during matches. In December 1977 Keegan was sent off for punching an opponent, who had repeatedly provoked him, as Hamburg met Lubeck in a supposed friendly match. Keegan received the second extended suspension of his career, with an eight week absence from the game. Keegan also felt the effects of the language barrier, before his efforts enabled him to master German. Keegan's positive attitude gradually won over his new team-mates, and he emerged as a star of the Hamburg team, helping them to win the Bundesliga in 1979. Keegan's growing ability as a player, demonstrated with Hamburg and England, led to him winning the European Footballer of the Year award in both 1978 and 1979.

During the 1979-80 season Keegan played a major role in Hamburg's progress to the European Cup Final. In the Second Round he scored in both legs as Dynamo Tbilisi were beaten twice. In the Semi Finals, Hamburg lost 2-0 against Real Madrid at the Santiago Bernabeu Stadium, but recovered to win their home leg 5-1, to take the tie 5-3 on aggregate, with Keegan having an outstanding match in the second leg. Hamburg returned to the Bernabeu stadium for the Final, where they met Nottingham Forest, who had beaten Malmo a year earlier to take the European Cup. Hamburg's main goalscorer, Horst Hrubesch, was not fully fit, but he was available as a substitute. Hamburg were managed by Branco Zebec, a Yugoslav who had played for Partizan Belgrade in the first ever European Cup match, twenty five years earlier. Ahead of the match Keegan was asked whether the Final would revolve around a duel between himself and Brian Clough. Keegan replied: "Not really. From where I am I might just be able to score a goal. From where he is sitting, he will find that very difficult". Hamburg dominated the early play, but Forest took the lead after twenty minutes, as John Robertson struck a low shot from just outside the penalty area, that fizzed into the net via a post. Hamburg thought they had equalised a minute later, but the effort from Reimann was ruled out by Antonio Garrido, the Portuguese referee, as a linesman flagged for offside against Keegan. Hamburg, for whom Hrubesch played the second half, continued to have most of the play for the remainder of the match, but Forest held on to win 1-0.

The success of English clubs in winning the European Cup was not matched at international level. England successively failed to reach the finals of the World Cups of 1974 and 1978, plus the European Championship of 1976. Qualification for the 1980 European Championship finals, staged in June of that year, was followed by the anti-climax of elimination in the group stage, while a hooligan element among the England supporters rioted in Italy. Keegan had scored seven times in the qualifiers, and played in each of England's three matches in the 1980 finals. The European title was won by West Germany, who beat Belgium 2-1 in the Final, with a couple of goals from the now fully-recovered Horst Hrubesch. Immediately after the tournament, Keegan left Hamburg, having arranged a surprise move to Southampton. In 1982 England appeared in the World Cup finals for the first time in twelve years, but Keegan was left on the sidelines, due to an injury. He managed only 27 minutes play, as a substitute, on football's highest stage, and headed wide when presented with an easy chance in England's 0-0 draw with Spain. Unfortunately that proved to be the end of Keegan's England playing days, as he was not selected by Bobby Robson, who replaced Ron Greenwood as manager that Summer. Keegan's club career, however, ended on a high note, as he helped Newcastle United win promotion from the Second Division in 1984.

After several years out of the limelight, living in Spain, Keegan returned to centre-stage in 1992, as manager of Newcastle. Keegan remained at Newcastle for five years, moulding an attacking team that finished as runners-up in the Premiership in both 1995-96 and 1996-97, but the pressures of the job led him to resign before the end of the latter season. Keegan therefore missed out on leading Newcastle's first European Cup campaign in 1997-98. He returned to club management in 1998 at Fulham, and then took the national manager's role in 1999, following the departure of Glenn Hoddle. Keegan led England to the Euro 2000 finals, where they beat Germany 1-0 – this being their first competitive win against either West Germany or Germany since the 1966 World Cup Final – but lost 3-2 against both Portugal and Romania. Later that year, a 1-0 defeat against Germany, in a World Cup qualifier – the last match played at Wembley Stadium, before it was demolished and rebuilt – prompted Keegan's immediate resignation. With refreshing honesty, Keegan admitted he lacked the tactical understanding required for success as an international manager. He departed saying "I have no complaints. I have not been quite good enough. I blame no one but myself".

Keegan soon bounced back, becoming manager of Manchester City, a club where he oversaw the same type of adventurous football as Newcastle played under his leadership. Manchester City won the First Division in 2001-02, Keegan's first season in charge, scoring 108 goals in 46 matches. City subsequently struggled in the Premiership, and Keegan left the club in March 2005. A return to Newcastle United in 2008 only lasted a few months, as a dispute with club owner, Mike Ashley, brought the departure of Keegan, who subsequently won a claim for unfair dismissal. Preferring television punditry to the pressures of club management, Keegan's next role, commencing in 2009, was with ESPN. Throughout the many changes of fortune in his career, Kevin Keegan has retained an enthusiastic and positive outlook. They are qualities that have led the football community to hold Keegan in very high regard.

7 Bryan Robson: Captain Marvel

Bryan Robson earned the nickname "Captain Marvel" with his performances on the football field in the 1980s. Robson led Manchester United back to glory, and acted as the inspiration for an England team which started to challenge for international honours, after both had been through decline in the 1970s. A combative midfielder, who played with bravery and great determination, Robson was plagued with injuries. In contrast to his competitive performances, Robson displayed a quiet and modest persona off field. After great achievements as a player, Robson has undertaken a series of managerial roles, including a spell as assistant coach of the England team, with mixed results.

He was born at Chester-le-Street, in Durham, on January 11 1957. As a child Bryan supported Newcastle United, regularly attending home matches with his father, Brian, who was a long-distance lorry driver. Bryan's playing abilities led him to become captain of the Chester-le-Street boys team, besides playing for his school team. At the age of thirteen he was given a trial by Burnley. Trials with Coventry City, Newcastle United, and West Bromwich Albion followed over the next couple of years. Robson joined West Brom as an apprentice in 1972, at the age of fifteen, being signed despite his lack of physical stature – he was 5 foot 7 inches tall and weighed seven stone – and was paid £6 per week. West Brom successfully built the young player's frame with a diet that included raw egg mixed with milk, sherry, and sugar for breakfast, and a bottle of beer each evening.

Robson turned professional in August 1974, and made his debut for West Brom in April 1975, when aged 18. Robson was given his chance by Don Howe, the West Brom manager, who was to subsequently say of the player's emergence: "He was small, but you can sense when a young man has something. Looking at him I thought he had got character, an inner confidence". In 1976 Robson met his future wife, Denise, buying her a drink in a pub when he learned that she was celebrating her twenty first birthday. "It wasn't really like me, chatting up a strange bird" he later reflected. Bryan and Denise were to have two daughters, Clare and Charlotte, followed by a son, Ben, during the 1980s. West Brom won promotion to the First Division at the end of 1975-76, but Robson's appearances the following season were limited by a freak sequence of three broken legs. After the first break, Robson attempted a quick return, via the reserves, and immediately suffered a fracture on the same leg. Later in the season, back in the first team, Robson broke the other leg. During 1978-79 Robson received his first taste of European football, as West Brom, now managed by Ron Atkinson, reached the Quarter Finals of the UEFA Cup. In October 1981, Robson moved to Manchester United, who paid a British record transfer fee of £1,500,000 for the player, who had made 243 senior appearances for West Brom, scoring 45 goals. Ron Atkinson, who had left West Brom to become United manager in June of that year, said: "It may seem a lot of money, but it's not even a gamble, you know. You're not even gambling with someone like him. This fella is solid gold". Robson had suddenly reached superstar status, with reputed earnings of £60,000 per year to match this.

Bryan Robson was by now a first choice for the national team. He had made his England debut on February 6 1980, as the Republic of Ireland were beaten 2-0 in a European Championship qualifier. Robson was included in the squad for the finals, staged in Italy during June, but did not get to play in the tournament. Between the Autumns of 1980 and 1981, Robson played in all eight of England's games in the 1982 World Cup qualifiers, scoring his first international goal in the infamous 2-1 defeat against Norway in September 1981. Robson provided an explosive start to England's first match in the World Cup finals, held in Spain during the Summer of 1982, scoring after just 27 seconds against France. Robson gave a brilliant display, directing operations in midfield, and scoring again later in the match, as England won 3-1. England followed this with victories against Czechoslovakia and Kuwait, but Robson missed the latter of these due to an injury. He returned for the second group stage, but England were now held to goalless draws by West Germany and Spain, and eliminated, despite being unbeaten in the tournament. A header from Robson which pulled a great save from Toni Schumacher was England's only real threat on goal against the Germans, while it was clever work by Robson that set up the chance from which Kevin Keegan sadly headed wide of an inviting goal against the Spaniards. England were managed in the World Cup finals by Ron Greenwood, who was about to retire from the role, with Don Howe and Geoff Hurst as assistants. Howe, who had overseen the start of Robson's career at West Brom, was criticised by many for having a negative influence on Greenwood's tactics, with his emphasis on defensive strength.

In October 1982 Robson was made captain of Manchester United, having established himself as an inspirational player with the club. In 1983 United won the FA Cup, beating Brighton and Hove Albion 4-0 in a replayed Final, with Robson scoring twice. The following season brought a run to the Semi Finals of the European Cup-Winners' Cup, with Robson orchestrating a famous 3-0 win against Barcelona, at Old Trafford, in the Quarter Finals, to wipe out a 2-0 defeat in the first leg. Robson scored twice as United outclassed a Barcelona team that featured Diego Maradona, and was chaired off the field by supporters, as thousands of United fans staged a good-natured pitch invasion. It was a moment that sealed an enduring bond between Robson and United, at a time when there was speculation he would be the subject of a multi-million pound transfer to one of a number of Italian clubs who coveted his ability. The FA Cup was regained in 1985, with United beating Everton in the Final, courtesy of a stunning goal from Norman Whiteside in extra time. Prior to this a combative Robson led the team's protests to the referee, Peter Willis, when Kevin Moran unluckily became the first player ever to be sent off in an FA Cup Final. Ron Atkinson believed that the FA Cup win in 1985 would be the starting point for Manchester United becoming the dominant club in England, but this did not happen. After winning their first ten League matches in 1985-86, United lost form as the season progressed, and eventually slumped to fourth place. Robson had several spells of absence due to injury this season, and only played in half of United's League matches.

Ron Greenwood was replaced as England manager by Bobby Robson, who was a great admirer of Bryan Robson. Bryan captained his country for the first time in November 1982, leading the team to a 3-0 win against Greece in a European Championship qualifier. England failed, however, to reach the 1984 European Championship finals, being eliminated by Denmark. Following this England impressed in winning their group in the 1986 World Cup qualifiers. Robson scored a hat trick as Turkey were beaten 8-0 in the Autumn of 1984. He also scored in the 5-0 win against Turkey at Wembley the following year, but Robson's commitment led to a pulled hamstring, as he chased a ball destined to go out of touch at a point when England were already five goals ahead. The finals, played in Mexico, arrived as Robson was struggling with a long-term shoulder injury. He dislocated the shoulder as England drew 0-0 with Morocco in their second match, and was left on the sidelines during the remainder of the campaign, which ended with defeat against Argentina in the Quarter Finals.

A poor start to the 1986-87 domestic season led to Ron Atkinson being sacked as Manchester United manager in November 1986. Atkinson remained an advocate for the brilliance of Robson in the following years, and paid the following tribute to the player in 1992: "Bryan is the complete midfield player. He deserves his nickname of 'Captain Marvel', because of his bravery and spirit, but he also has great skill and a deep understanding of the game. I put him up there with the all-time greats like Dave MacKay and Duncan Edwards. Bryan drives a team. A lot of players look to him for inspiration. His personal courage is staggering and he is a born leader. I have seen him tear a strip off superstar team-mates if they weren't doing their stuff, and I have seen him orchestrate the flow of play on the field with the subtlest of hand signals. There is nobody you would rather have out on the park as team captain. The factor that is most striking about Bryan is his competitive nature. He is special on the field, and down-to-earth and pleasant off it". The new United manager, Alex Ferguson, aimed high, but was initially unable to deliver real success. Robson remained a central figure as captain, and United finished as runners-up in the League in 1988, but were consigned to mid-table positions in 1987, 1989, and 1990. The last of these years, however, saw United win a trophy for the first time since 1985, as Robson captained the club to a third FA Cup victory in the space of seven years, with Crystal Palace being beaten in a replayed Final.

Robson was now nearing the end of his England career. In 1988 he had scored a fine goal against the Netherlands in the European Championship finals, but England lost that match 3-1. Indeed they were beaten in all three of their matches in the finals. In December 1989, a few weeks after England had achieved qualification for the following year's World Cup finals, Robson scored what was then the fastest goal in a first-class match at Wembley, finding the net after 38 seconds in England's 2-1 win against Yugoslavia – Robson also scored his team's other goal in this victory. The 1990 World Cup finals, hosted by Italy, proved to be a frustrating repeat of 1986 for Robson. He was substituted in England's second match, a goalless draw against the Netherlands, due to an ankle injury, and returned home early. Fourteen years after the event, Paul Gascoigne claimed in his autobiography that Robson's departure was sealed by a further injury, as he gashed a toe during a drinking session at the team hotel after the match. In *Robbo: My Autobiography*, published in 2006, Robson denied this, saying that Gascoigne accepted his memory was mistaken. Robson's role as a battling midfielder was taken on by David Platt, and England went on to reach the Semi Finals, where they lost to West Germany on penalties.

Bobby Robson's tenure as England manager ended with the 1990 finals. In *Against the Odds: An Autobiography*, which was published later in 1990, Bobby Robson (caught between the past and present tenses) paid the following tribute to Bryan: "He is a truly amazing player; the bravest, most committed, strongest I ever had. He could do everything and did so for England. He has heart and industry, he could win the ball, pass it, score goals, play off other people brilliantly, read a situation before it developed, and could time his runs into opponents' penalty areas to absolute perfection. He was a wonderful inspiration and could lift sides on his own efforts – not by what he said, but by what he did". Graham Taylor, the next England manager, was less of an enthusiast about Bryan Robson. Intermittent appearances under Taylor saw Robson play his final England match in October 1991, as Turkey were beaten 1-0 in a European Championship qualifier. During an international career lasting eleven years, Robson had made 90 appearances for England, 65 of them as captain, and scored 26 goals.

As the years passed, it appeared that Robson would not fulfil his true potential. Besides his disappointments at international tournaments with England, Robson's Manchester United had failed to win the League, and been denied some opportunities to compete in Europe by the post-Heysel ban on English clubs. In 1990-91 Manchester United took part in the European Cup-Winners' Cup, upon the re-admittance of English clubs to Europe. United went on to win the trophy, beating Barcelona 2-1 in the 1991 Final, at Rotterdam, with Robson setting up the chances that led to both of United's goals. He later recalled this as a highlight of his football career: "Looking back over more than 400 games with Manchester United fills me with deep delight and few things have given me more pleasure in life than lifting the European Cup-Winners' Cup. That 1991 victory against Barcelona would rate as one of my finest performances for United".

Manchester United looked set to win the League in 1992, but a drop in form at the end of the season caused them to be edged out by Leeds United, while Robson missed several games due to a calf injury. United won both the European Super Cup and the League Cup Final in 1991-92, but Robson did not appear in either match. In 1992-93 Manchester United won the Premier League in its inaugural season, thereby becoming English champions for the first time since 1967. Robson, who reached the age of 36 midway through the season, was no longer able to command a regular place in the team, being limited to 14 appearances in the Premier League. He did, however, make a great contribution with a series of substitute appearances during the winning run that clinched the title, including the famous 2-1 victory against Sheffield Wednesday, clinched with two late goals from Steve Bruce. As Robson entered the twilight of his playing career, United finally embarked upon a period of dominance of the English game. They won the Premiership and FA Cup double in 1994. Robson made 15 league appearances this season, but did not feature in the victory against Chelsea in the FA Cup Final – although he had scored against Oldham Athletic in the Semi Final replay. Robson played his final match for United in May 1994, as the Premiership season ended with a 0-0 draw against Coventry City. During more than twelve years with the club, Robson had played 459 senior matches for Manchester United, scoring 99 goals.

During the Summer of 1994 Robson moved to Middlesbrough, becoming player-manager. His first season in this role was a success, as Middlesbrough won the First Division in the Spring of 1995. Robson combined his role at Middlesbrough with that of assistant to Terry Venables, who had been appointed as England coach in 1994. Venables and Robson completed their spell with England at the Euro 96 finals. Amidst national euphoria the home country's team reached the Semi Finals, only to lose to Germany on penalties. At Middlesbrough Robson and the chairman Steve Gibson, whose working relationship merged with a close friendship, succeeded in attracting a series of international stars to the previously unfashionable club. Players lured to Middlesbrough in the wake of success included Juninho, Branco, Emerson (each from Brazil), Fabrizio Ravenelli (Italy), Christian Ziege (Germany), Christian Karembeu (France), and Alen Boksic (Croatia).

In 1996-97 a remarkable season saw Middlesbrough reach the Finals of the League Cup and the FA Cup, only to lose both of them, against Leicester City and Chelsea respectively, while also being relegated from the Premiership. Relegation was sealed by the deduction of three points, this being the FA sanction for Middlesbrough unilaterally postponing a match against Blackburn

Rovers, in December, when most of their squad were laid-low by illness or injury. Robson retired from the playing squad in January 1998, at the age of 41 – having made his final appearance against Arsenal, in the Premiership, on New Year's Day 1997. As manager, Robson led the club back to the Premiership at the first attempt, with promotion at the end of 1997-98. Middlesbrough also reached the League Cup Final in 1998, but lost to Chelsea.

At the end of 2000, with Middlesbrough struggling in the Premiership, Robson was joined by Terry Venables, the coach he had supported in the England role a few years previously. Middlesbrough escaped possible relegation at the end of the 2000-01 season, but Robson resigned, feeling that the club had lost confidence in him. Robson was now thanked for his efforts by Steve Gibson, who said: "When he came, the club had never progressed beyond the sixth round of the FA Cup. We were perceived as a yo-yo club. He took us to a semi-final of an FA Cup, we won the semi-final and went to Wembley. We've been in the Premier League for five years and we were in the Nationwide League Division One for two. We came up as champions on one occasion and were promoted automatically on the other. We have a 35,000-seat stadium and a world-class training ground. Bryan has attracted world-class players to the club. It has been a superb and wonderful and extremely pleasurable time".

Over the next couple of years Robson worked as a television pundit, while also having a small role in the training set-up at Manchester United. In October 2003 the Nigeria Football Association looked set to appoint Robson as coach of their national team, but did not proceed, due to significant opposition within the country to the appointment of a foreign coach. Robson returned to management, however, the following month, at Bradford City. Bradford were in the relegation zone when Robson arrived, and dropped out of the First Division in the Spring of 2004, whereupon Robson departed from the club. He soon took up another relegation struggle. In November 2004 Robson returned to West Brom, the club he had begun with as a player, being appointed manager. Robson proved an inspirational figure, and at the end of 2004-05 West Brom became the first team in the thirteen seasons of the Premiership to avoid relegation after being bottom at Christmas, edging ahead of Crystal Palace, Norwich City, and Southampton after a compelling tussle. The magic did not last, however, as a year later West Brom were relegated from the Premiership. A poor start in the Championship the following season saw Robson leave the club, in September 2006. He returned to management at Sheffield United, another Championship club, in 2007, but left early in the following year, following acrimony with both players and fans. In March 2008, fourteen years after leaving Manchester United as a player, Robson was appointed as an ambassador for the club. In the Autumn of 2009, he took on the new challenge of managing the national team of Thailand. Robson's tenure did not prove a real success, and he left the role in 2011, with the team having failed to reach the finals of the Asian Cup. Robson was by now facing a much more important battle, having been diagnosed with throat cancer. Having undergone an operation in March 2011, Robson made a good recovery over the next few months.

8 Diego Maradona: Master Inspirer of Dreams

Diego Maradona is most commonly remembered in Britain for the goals he scored as Argentina beat England in the 1986 World Cup finals. Maradona's two goals in that match, scored only a few minutes apart, symbolise a career in which controversy mingled with brilliance. The first goal was the infamous handled effort, while the second saw Maradona score one of the greatest goals in the history of football. Despite a career blighted by bans for drug taking, Maradona is revered as one of the greatest ever footballers, due to the amazing quality of his play, which was a major factor in Argentina winning the 1986 World Cup, and finishing as runners-up four years later. Although standing at just 5 feet and 6 inches, Maradona had enormous physical strength, which was allied with great pace and balance. He was an attacking midfielder who scored many goals, a free kick specialist, and a brilliant dribbler. As a team captain, Maradona motivated team-mates with his great will to win. Apart from bouts of gamesmanship, his only weakness on the field of play appeared to be an over-reliance on his left foot – he was never comfortable shooting with his right foot.

Diego Armando Maradona was born on October 30 1960, in Buenos Aires, the fifth of eight children of another Diego Maradona, a factory worker, and his wife, Dalma. Diego's childhood was characterised by poverty, with the family living in a three room house, which lacked running water, in the Villa Fiorito district of Buenos Aires. Diego played football incessantly on the local waste ground, and developed an amazing talent. At the age of nine he was given a trial by Argentinos Juniors, and accepted into the club's youth programme. Maradona made his first team debut in the Argentinian league in October 1976, at age of only 15. With their prospects improving due to Diego's success, his family now moved to a better home. The following year saw Maradona gain a place in Argentina's national team, making his debut as a substitute in a 5-1 win against Hungary on February 27 1977. Later that year Maradona began a relationship with Claudia Villafane, who was literally the girl next door – it would prove to be the great romance of his life.

Diego was included in Argentina's provisional squad of 25 players for the 1978 World Cup finals, but omitted from the final 22. The coach, Cesar Luis Menotti, thought that Maradona, now aged 17, lacked the required experience. Maradona later described his omission as "the biggest disappointment of my life". Argentina went on to win the 1978 World Cup, beating the Netherlands 3-1 in the Final, with Maradona among the 77,000 crowd at the Monumental Stadium, in his home city. Shortly afterwards Harry Haslam, the manager of Sheffield United, made an audacious attempt to buy Maradona for the Second Division club, during a visit to Argentina. Haslam agreed a £200,000 transfer fee with Argentinos Juniors, but Sheffield United were unable to meet this cost, choosing instead to buy Alejandro Sabella from River Plate for £160,000. Sabella flourished in England, although failing to reach the heights of Osvaldo Ardiles and Ricardo Villa, two members of the Argentina team who joined Tottenham Hotspur a few weeks after the 1978 World Cup finals.

Maradona was rapidly offered a series of advertising deals, which he eagerly accepted. The young player endorsed high-profile brands, including Agfa, Coca-Cola, and Puma. Maradona scored his first goal for Argentina in a 3-1 win against Scotland, at Glasgow, in June 1979. A few weeks later he played for his country in the Copa America. Maradona then captained Argentina at the World Youth Cup, held in Japan during August and September, and won his first honour, as the Soviet Union were beaten 3-1 in the Final, in which Maradona scored. His emergence on the international stage led to Maradona winning the 1979 South American Footballer of the Year award, organised by *El Mundo* of Caracas. He would subsequently win the award again in 1980, 1986, 1989, 1990, and 1992.

In May 1980 Maradona gave a great display for Argentina against England, at Wembley, but the world champions lost 3-1. Maradona moved from Argentinos Juniors to Boca Juniors in February 1981, and helped his new club win the Argentinian league title that year. Boca were managed by Silvio Marzolini, who had played for Argentina against England in both the 1962 and 1966 World Cup finals. In the Summer of 1982, Maradona appeared in the World Cup finals for the first time, as Argentina defended their title in Spain. The start of the tournament coincided with Argentina's military defeat against Britain in the Falklands War. A dispirited Argentinian football team struggled in Spain. After losing 1-0 to Belgium in the opening match, Argentina recovered to beat Hungary 4-1, with a shining Maradona scoring twice, and El Salvador 2-0. The second group phase brought frustration and defeat. Maradona was the victim of some tough marking by Claudio Gentile in the 2-1 reverse against Italy, and was sent off for a terrible foul on Batista as Argentina lost 3-1 against Brazil.

Immediately after the finals, Maradona joined Barcelona, in a £1,875,000 transfer, and was soon joined by Menotti as manager. In December 1982 Maradona was struck with hepatitis, an illness that kept him out of action for three months. At the end of the 1982-83 season, Maradona appeared for Barcelona as they won 2-1 against Real Madrid – managed by Alfredo Di Stefano – in the Spanish Cup Final. September 1983 brought another halt to Maradona's career, as he suffered a fractured ankle, inflicted by a vicious tackle from Andoni Goicoechea, known as the "Butcher of Bilbao", as Barcelona beat Athletic Bilbao. Maradona recovered quickly, and returned to competitive football in January 1984. Barcelona reached the Cup Final again this season, but lost a bruising encounter against Athletic Bilbao 1-0. Besides the couple of enforced absences from the team, Maradona endured a lot of frustration at Barcelona, and frequent clashes with Jose Luis Nunez, the club President. Maradona later admitted that during his spell with Barcelona he started to take drugs. Maradona moved to Napoli in the Summer of 1984. They were a struggling Serie A club at this point, and spent the first half of the 1984-85 season in the relegation zone, before climbing in the latter months. Inspired by Maradona, Napoli's revival continued in 1985-86, and they finished in third place.

Back in January 1983, when Maradona had been at living quietly at Lloret de Mar, near Barcelona, recovering from hepatitis, his career received a great boost as Carlos Bilardo, the new Argentinian manager, visited and asked him to be captain of the national team. Bilardo had played for the notorious Estudiantes de La Plata team which hacked its way to victory against Manchester United in the 1968 World Club Championship. Maradona enthusiastically took up the new role, initially only as a figurehead, as he did not actually captain Argentina on the field until 1985, with Bilardo basing the national team on home-based players during the intervening period. Maradona led Argentina through a successful campaign in the qualifiers for the 1986 World Cup, but suffered a severe knee injury when he was kicked by a hooligan in Venezuela, during May 1985.

The 1986 World Cup finals, in Mexico, saw Maradona, now aged 25, reach the apex of his career, as captain of an outstanding Argentina team that won the trophy, being unbeaten in seven matches. In the group stage, Argentina beat South Korea 3-1 and Bulgaria 2-0, either side of a 1-1 draw with Italy in which Maradona scored. In the Second Round, Argentina beat Uruguay 1-0, with Maradona, who was unlucky not to score with a thirty yard free kick which hit the crossbar, in rampant form. In the Quarter Finals, Maradona scored twice, early in the second half, as England were beaten 2-1. The first goal saw Maradona go unpunished for punching the ball into the net – immediately after the match he said the goal was scored by "a little bit of the hand of God, another bit by the head of Maradona" The second goal was a brilliant solo effort, as Maradona received the ball just inside the Argentinian half, and set off on an irresistible run, beating four English players at great pace, before taking the ball around the advancing Peter Shilton, and slotting it into the net. Maradona again scored twice in the space of a few minutes, as Belgium were beaten 2-0 in the Semi Finals. For his second goal against the Belgians, Maradona made a powerful run in which he evaded four opponents, before striking an unstoppable shot. In the Final, Argentina beat West Germany 3-2, with Maradona having a role in the creation of each of his team's goals. During his retirement, Maradona recalled the victory as "The most sublime moment of my career. When I was there with the World Cup in my hands, I felt I was touching the sky. All my dreams had come true". After collecting the trophy, Maradona said he wished to dedicate the World Cup victory to those children in the world who were poor, just as he had been, hoping that Argentina's success had brought "a little happiness into their lives".

Immediately after the World Cup finals, Diego enjoyed a holiday with Claudia in Polynesia. Following this Maradona enjoyed real success in Europe for the first time, being instrumental in Napoli winning the Italian title for the first time in their history at the end of the 1986-87 season. Napoli also won the Italian Cup that season, beating Atalanta 4-0 on aggregate in the Final. Off the pitch, this was also a great time for Diego Maradona, with Claudia giving birth to Dalma, their first daughter, on April 2 1987. Diego and Claudia's second daughter, Giannina, followed on May 16 1989, and the couple got married later that year, fully twelve years after the start of their relationship. The happy family image was undermined, however, by a long-running paternity case, as Cristiana Sinagra, an Italian woman with whom he had an affair, claimed Maradona was the father of her son. The Italian courts finally ruled this to be the case in 1993, and the player subsequently accepted his parentage of the son, who took the name Diego Maradona Junior, and began a professional football career with Genoa.

Maradona began to talk of Napoli's success in terms of a political allegory, with the team from the poor south of Italy, supported by the workers, but despised by wealthy and powerful forces in Rome and Milan, succeeding through a great will to win. Maradona's championing of working class football seemed to be at odds with his revelling in a millionaire lifestyle during his time in Italy. He signed advertising contracts for a wide variety of products, including sports clothing – Hitochi paying him USD 5,000,000 for this – beer, coffee, stationery, and sweets. Maradona indulged a love of fast cars, with manufacturers giving him their latest models in the hope of benefiting from association with the player. He once asked for a Mercedes Benz, only to turn away the car when it arrived, as it was an automatic. Maradona became a darling of the media, with his own programme on Italian television. A poll by the International Management Group concluded that Maradona was the best-known person in the world. IMG opportunistically offered Maradona USD 100,000,000 for his image rights, on condition that he take dual nationality as a citizen of the USA as well as Argentina. Maradona, whose staunch patriotism for Argentina has always been a guiding force, flatly refused the idea.

In June and July 1987 Maradona led Argentina, as host nation, in the Copa America, despite struggling with a fever. A tremendous personal display by Maradona could not prevent a 1-0 defeat against Uruguay in the Semi Finals, following which Argentina lost 2-1 against Colombia in a Third Place match that was particularly obscure – thick fog shrouded the Monumental Stadium, where a crowd of only 15,000 had gathered. In August 1987, little more than a year after the "Hand of God" incident, Maradona played at Wembley for a Rest of the World team that lost 3-0 against the Football League, in a match to mark the centenary of the Football League. A sizeable segment of the crowd barracked Maradona throughout the match, but others appreciated his brilliant midfield partnership with Michel Platini.

Back in Italy, Napoli were runners-up in Serie A in both 1988 and 1989. In 1989 Napoli won the UEFA Cup, beating Stuttgart 5-4 on aggregate in the Final, with Maradona among the scorers, but lost 4-1 on aggregate against Sampdoria in the Italian Cup Final. In July 1989 Maradona led Argentina in the Copa America, staged in Brazil, with the team being restricted to third place. Maradona, who was now showing signs of waywardness, stayed in South America for several weeks after the tournament, missing the start of the 1989-90 season with Napoli. After five years of high-pressure football in Italy, Maradona was looking for a change, while his image had been tarnished by suggestions that he was associated with the Neapolitan Mafia. After his reluctant return, Maradona played a major role in Napoli regaining the Italian title in the Spring of 1990.

Maradona captained Argentina at the 1990 World Cup finals, staged in Italy. The campaign opened with a humiliating 1-0 defeat against Cameroon, but a team inspired by Maradona somehow managed to overcome a series of lacklustre displays to reach the Final. A piece of Maradona magic conjured up a goal for Claudio Caniggia, as Brazil were beaten 1-0, very much against the run of play, in the Second Round. In the Quarter Finals, Yugoslavia were beaten on penalties, following a 0-0 draw after extra time, despite Maradona's effort in the penalty contest being saved. A bitter clash against Italy in the Semi Finals – held at Napoli's stadium – was drawn 1-1, after extra time, following which Argentina won on penalties, with Maradona this time among the scorers in the penalty contest. Argentina came unstuck against West Germany in the Final, losing an awful match 1-0, as Andy Brehme scored from a disputed penalty late in the match. A free kick from Maradona in the first half was Argentina's only attempt on goal in the Final, while the team had Pedro Monzon and Gustavo Dezotti sent off. Following the final whistle, Maradona was soon in tears, as he reflected upon his shattered dream of leading Argentina to a second World Cup triumph. Later that year, Maradona announced his retirement from the international team.

Maradona's role in the elimination of Italy from the World Cup further soured the love affair between the player and Napoli. Maradona scored twice as Napoli beat Ujpest Dozsa 5-0 on aggregate in the First Round of the 1990-91 European Cup. He initially refused to join the team as they travelled to the Soviet Union for a match against Spartak Moscow in the following round, before changing his mind, and arriving by private jet, but Napoli were eliminated on penalties. In March 1991 Maradona tested positive for cocaine, after playing for Napoli in a 1-0 win against Bari. This led to a fifteen month worldwide ban on Maradona playing football, imposed by FIFA. Maradona spent the period of his ban in Argentina, and was arrested for use of cocaine shortly after his return, but managed to play in a few charity football matches.

When he became eligible to play again, Maradona wished to avoid a return to Napoli. After protracted negotiations, Seville, who were managed by Bilardo, bought Maradona from Napoli in 1992. Maradona failed to perform effectively for Seville, and he was sacked by the club in the Summer of 1993, after a furious row with Bilardo. Maradona then returned to play his football in Argentina, joining Newell's Old Boys in September. Despite his troubles at Seville, Maradona returned to Argentina's national team, being persuaded to do so by Alfio Basile, who had replaced Bilardo as manager. Maradona's first match for Argentina since the 1990 World Cup finals was a 1-1 draw with Brazil, at Buenos Aires, in February 1993. The match was staged to celebrate the centenary of Argentina's Football Association. At a commemorative banquet the previous day, Maradona had been officially lauded as Argentina's greatest ever footballer. He sportingly suggested that Di Stefano had been better. Maradona missed most of Argentina's matches in the 1994 World Cup qualifiers, but helped them beat Australia, in a two legged play-off in the latter part of 1993, to secure a place in the finals. In the domestic game, fitness problems, and disputes with the club, led to another abrupt departure for Maradona, as he was sacked by Newell's Old Boys in February 1994. With a large group of journalists outside his home, seeking details of his departure, an angry Maradona fired an air rifle at them, causing injuries to four of the reporters. There were fears for Maradona's mental as well as his physical health. He was eventually given a conviction for the air rifle incident in 2002, and a suspended two year jail sentence.

Despite lacking a club, Maradona remained part of the national team set up during the early months of 1994, as he battled to regain fitness ahead of the World Cup finals. Maradona's apparent recovery gave way to a further downfall at the finals, staged in the USA. He scored as Argentina beat Greece 4-0 in their first match, and directed a memorable celebration to a camera near the pitch. The 2-1 win against Nigeria in the next match proved to be the end of Maradona's World Cup career, as he tested positive for a cocktail of performance-enhancing drugs. He was suspended from the remainder of the tournament, and Argentina departed in the Second Round, losing 3-2 to Romania. FIFA rapidly handed Maradona his second fifteen month ban from football in the space of three years. This spelt the end of a remarkable international journey, stretching (with several intervals) across seventeen years from 1977 to 1994, in which Maradona had played 90 matches for Argentina, and scored 33 goals. Maradona had played 21 of these matches in the World Cup finals of 1982, 1986, 1990, and 1994, during which he scored eight times.

Although banned from playing, Maradona was allowed to take up coaching roles with clubs in Argentina. A spell with Mandiyu during 1994 ended with Maradona and the club owner having a flaming row in the dressing room. At Racing in 1995, Maradona left in support of the outgoing club president. Following this Pele attempted to broker a move to Santos for Maradona, but the latter had set his heart on finishing his playing career with Boca Juniors. Maradona's old club re-acquired him and, with his suspension having expired, he returned to the playing field at the end of September 1995. Around this time, Maradona was busy on several fronts. Earlier in September, at Paris, Maradona founded the World Union of Footballers, with Eric Cantona being the other leading participant. In November 1995, Maradona visited Oxford University, having been invited to speak to the Oxford Union, and was accorded the title "Master Inspirer of Dreams". January 1996 saw Maradona, who publicly admitted to still being an addict, help launch an anti-drugs campaign, led by Carlos Menem, the President of Argentina.

Maradona was soon joined at Boca Juniors by Carlos Bilardo, who replaced Silvio Marzolini, another face from the past, as manager. Maradona showed flashes of his old brilliance during this swan-song, but addiction to cocaine continued to trouble him, with a spell at a clinic in Switzerland during 1996 failing to produce a cure. Maradona finally retired from football in 1997, playing his final match for Boca Juniors on October 25, a few days before his thirty seventh birthday, at a time when he faced a probable third suspension for drug taking, having recently tested positive for cocaine. It was a sad end to an amazing football career that had begun twenty one years earlier.

The immediate sequel was that Maradona suffered an alarming physical decline, as he put on a lot of weight after losing the discipline of keeping fit to play football, while continuing to use drugs. In January 2000 he was admitted to hospital in Uruguay, having suffered a heart attack due to continued use of cocaine. Maradona moved to Cuba, where he received extensive treatment for his health problems, and developed a strong friendship with Fidel Castro. Maradona's marriage with Claudia collapsed, and the couple were divorced in 2004. In April of that year, a few weeks after returning to live in Argentina, Maradona was admitted to hospital, suffering from breathing difficulties. Maradona returned to Cuba in September 2004, for treatment of his cocaine addiction. This was followed by a stomach-stapling operation in Colombia during March 2005, which helped Maradona lose four stone in three months. In May 2005 Maradona, looking fairly fit, attended the Champions League Final, in which Liverpool beat Milan on penalties. The opening goal of the match was scored by Paolo Maldini, who had coincidentally paid tribute to Maradona in a recent interview. When asked who was the best player he faced in his long career, Maldini, regarded as a saint in Italian football, had surprisingly said: "Diego Maradona was not only the greatest, but also the most honest. He was a model of good behaviour on the pitch. He was respectful of everyone, from the great players down to the ordinary team member. He was always getting kicked around, and he never complained – not like some of today's strikers". The rejuvenation of Maradona continued back in Argentina in August 2005, as he began to host a chat show on television. A return to football saw Maradona being active in a vice president role at Boca Juniors, during 2005 and 2006. A recurrence of health problems led to Maradona being treated in hospital during 2007 for hepatitis and alcohol abuse.

In 2008 Maradona was appointed coach of Argentina, despite not having had any coaching experience since 1995. The hope appeared to be that his legendary status, and charisma, would motivate the players. In his first match as coach, Maradona's Argentina beat Scotland 1-0, at Hampden Park, the scene of his first international goal. The following year Argentina suffered a 6-1 defeat against Bolivia in a World Cup qualifier, but they recovered in subsequent matches to gain a place in the finals. In South Africa, during 2010, Argentina defeated Nigeria, South Korea, and Greece in the group stage. In the Second Round, Argentina beat Mexico 3-1, with Carlos Tevez scoring twice. Maradona directed the team from the technical area, alternating between hyperactivity and frustration. Realistic hopes of Argentina winning the World Cup crashed with a 4-0 humiliation by Germany in the Quarter Finals. A few weeks later, the Argentinian federation announced that Maradona's contract was not being renewed. During the following year Maradona took an unexpected new coaching role, at Al Wasl, a club from the United Arab Emirates.

Following his retirement from the playing field, Maradona had written a fascinating autobiography, *El Diego*, published in 2000, a year in which he and Pele were jointly lauded by FIFA as the greatest players of the twentieth century. A semi-update of Maradona's book appeared in 2004. Maradona vividly celebrated his amazing achievements, and admitted many weaknesses. His impassioned narrative displayed a personality that has always been a strange combination of arrogance and paranoia. Maradona was open about having taken drugs through most of his football career, but claimed to have been clean on each of the three occasions he tested positive. Amidst all the complexities and contradictions, Maradona's love of football shone brightly. As he surveyed his life, Maradona enthused: "I always wanted to play football. All I wanted was to run after the ball, to get hold of it, to play. Playing football gave me a unique peace. And that same sensation has been with me always, even today: give me a ball and I'll have fun. I'll stand my ground, I'll tussle. I'll want to win, and I'll want to play well. Give me a ball and let me do what I know best, anywhere. True, people are important and people motivate you but people are not on the pitch. And that's where the fun is: on the pitch with the ball. That's what I've always done, whether at Wembley or the Maracana, with a hundred thousand people watching. And that's what we did in Fiorito".

9 Gary Lineker: Everything I Could Want Out of Life

Gary Lineker is one of the great gentlemen of modern English football. During a playing career in which he was never booked, Lineker displayed great sportsmanship, modesty, and humour. Despite winning relatively few honours, Lineker built a great reputation, as a prolific goalscorer in both domestic and international football. His apparently simple goalscoring style belied the effort he put into his game. Lineker's work-rate, and running off the ball, made him a player who had to be seen live to appreciate his full ability.

Lineker was born on November 30 1960, at Leicester. As a child, Gary's twin passions were football and cricket, with the ambition of becoming a professional in one of these sports. He has recalled "In the Summer I used to go mad on cricket, then the Winter would come again and it was all football, playing in the garden every night with my brother. Every spare moment was football". In 1969 Gary made his first trip to Wembley, seeing Leicester City play Manchester City in the FA Cup Final. A 1-0 defeat for Leicester was followed by a tearful journey home for Gary, aged eight at the time. Leicester's goalkeeper that day was Peter Shilton, with whom Lineker was destined to play for England, at Wembley, and many other venues around the world.

Gary's dedication to football was rewarded during his teenage years, as he was taken on as an apprentice by Leicester City. Gary also worked on his family's stall at Leicester market. The market stall was soon left behind, as Gary signed professional terms with Leicester City, and made his first team debut in 1978-79. Leicester won the Second Division title the following season, but Lineker's role was restricted to three goals in 19 League appearances. He remained a fringe player the following season, while Leicester were immediately relegated from the First Division. From 1981-82 onwards, however, Lineker was almost ever-present in the Leicester team, and a frequent scorer of goals, peaking with 26 League strikes in 1982-83, a season in which Leicester won promotion. Lineker eventually scored 95 goals in 194 League matches at Leicester, a record that led to his being bought by Everton, who had just won the League, in the Summer of 1985, for a fee of £800,000.

Lineker was given his England debut by Bobby Robson in May 1984, appearing as a substitute in the 1-1 draw against Scotland. His next appearance for England was in the starting line-up against the Republic of Ireland in March 1985, and he scored in the 2-1 win.

Three months later he netted twice in a 5-0 win against the USA. Lineker was a prolific goalscorer for Everton, finishing the 1985-86 season as the First Division's leading marksman, with thirty goals. This led to his winning both the Footballer of the Year award (from the Football Writers' Association) and the Player of the Year award (from the Professional Footballers' Association). Everton's season, however, ended in disappointment, as they were runners-up to Liverpool in both the League and FA Cup. Lineker opened the scoring in the FA Cup Final, but Liverpool recovered to win 3-1.

Lineker played in four of England's eight matches in the 1986 World Cup qualifiers, and scored a hat trick in the 5-0 win against Turkey, in October 1985, that secured a place in the finals. A week before the start of the finals, Lineker suffered a wrist injury as England beat Canada 1-0 in a warm-up match. It initially appeared he might be unfit for the tournament, but he was able to play, with the wrist strapped. England made a slow start to the finals, losing 1-0 to Portugal and drawing 0-0 with Morocco, before exploding into life with a 3-0 win against Poland, in which Lineker scored a hat trick in the first thirty six minutes. Lineker then netted twice in the 3-0 win against Paraguay. The other goal came from Peter Beardsley, this being the only England goal in the 1986 finals which was not scored by Lineker, who was off the pitch at the time, receiving treatment after being elbowed in the throat by a Paraguayan. In the Quarter Finals two goals from Diego Maradona secured victory for Argentina, but only after a late fightback from England, in which Lineker scored once, and was inches away from adding an equaliser. Lineker's six goal haul won him the Golden Boot as the tournament's leading scorer.

Following the World Cup finals, Lineker moved from Everton, after just a year at the club, being bought by Barcelona, who were managed by Terry Venables, for a fee of £2,750,000. Lineker immediately established himself at Barcelona, scoring 21 league goals in 1986-87, including a hat trick in a 3-2 win against Real Madrid, but at the end of the season it was Real who won the title, with Barcelona finishing second in league. Lineker made great efforts to fit in at Barcelona, and learned Spanish along with his wife, Michelle (something which required perseverance on their part). His ability to conduct interviews with the media in Spanish, and his embracing of local culture (in contrast with several English players with continental clubs), won Lineker a lot of popularity in Spain. Venables left Barcelona in 1987, and became manager of Tottenham Hotspur.

Barcelona, now managed by Carlos Rexach, won the Spanish Cup in 1988, beating Real Sociedad 1-0 in the Final, enabling Lineker to win his first club trophy since Leicester won the Second Division eight years earlier.

At international level, Lineker established a reputation as a deadly goalscorer. He scored five goals in England's qualifying matches for the 1988 European Championship – the total being bolstered by his second hat trick against Turkey, who were beaten 8-0 in October 1987. Even more spectacularly, Lineker scored four times as Spain were beaten 4-2 in a friendly, at Madrid, in February 1987. England flopped at the 1988 European Championship finals, in West Germany, losing all three of their matches. In contrast to his success in the World Cup two years earlier, Lineker failed to score in this tournament, and looked out of touch. Within a few days the reason for this emerged, as Lineker found himself in hospital, being treated for a previously undiagnosed attack of hepatitis.

Johan Cruyff became manager of Barcelona in the Summer of 1988. Rexach had started to use Lineker in a withdrawn role on the right wing, rather than as a striker, and Cruyff continued this approach. During 1988-89 Lineker ceased to be an automatic choice in the Barcelona team, and only scored six goals. Barcelona finished as runners-up in the Spanish league this season, but won the European Cup-Winners' Cup, beating Sampdoria 2-0 in the Final. Lineker set up the first goal, scored by Julio Salinas – with a cross from the right. Prior to this Lineker had scored in four of Barcelona's matches in the European campaign, including both legs of the Semi Final against CFKA Sredets (a temporary name for CSKA Sofia). The Cup-Winners' Cup victory was to prove the greatest honour Lineker won as a club player. He never won a league title, and also missed out on playing in the European Cup when Everton were prevented from appearing in the 1985-86 competition, as reigning champions, due to the post-Heysel ban on English clubs.

Lineker returned to English domestic football in the Summer of 1989, joining Tottenham Hotspur, thereby linking up again with Terry Venables. Lineker played in all 38 of Spurs' First Division matches as they took third place in 1989-90, and emerged as the division's leading scorer with 24 goals. On the pitch, Lineker built up a great understanding with the young Paul Gascoigne. Off the pitch, Lineker was a target for Gascoigne's delight in wind-ups. After Lineker invited Gascoigne to his home, described by the latter as being situated "in a very posh Georgian terrace in St John's Wood", Gazza (who lived in Hertfordshire) took to regularly parking his car on Lineker's front drive, without permission, on trips to London. More importantly than living in a posh house, Gary Lineker has always enjoyed, and appreciated, the life that football has given him. A few weeks before the 1990 World Cup finals, when being interviewed by Pete Davies for the book *All Played Out: The Full Story of Italia '90*, Lineker reflected upon his experiences up to that point: "I know I am lucky. Touch wood, everything I've done in my life has been what I wanted to do, workwise, and my health's been good. Health's the main thing. If you've got that, then you're OK. I've had everything I could want out of life. Everything I've done has surprised me. When I joined Leicester as an apprentice, I always wanted to do that, but I didn't really think I would. Then I signed as a professional, and I thought, well I didn't think they'd take me on. Then I played in the first team. Everything that came was more than I'd ever hoped for. Then it went to being top scorer in the World Cup, and playing for Barcelona. I mean, all those things, if I'd been told even a year before they happened, I just wouldn't have believed it. I wouldn't have dared dream it. It's difficult to explain how you actually feel. It's a bit of self-doubt in a way. I think I know a bit more what I'm at now, what I can do, after doing it so many years, but there's a lot of luck involved".

In the 1990 World Cup qualifiers, Lineker scored for England in victories against both Albania and Poland. England's first match in the World Cup finals opened with Lineker scoring a typical opportunist goal against the Republic of Ireland after eight minutes, but the match ended as a 1-1 draw. He subsequently scored twice in the dramatic 3-2 win against Cameroon in the Quarter Finals, coolly equalising from a penalty late in normal time, before scoring a further goal from the spot in extra time. After the match Gary said that, as he prepared to take the first of the penalties, he composed himself by thinking about his brother Wayne, who was in Tenerife – Wayne owned Linekers Bar, at Playa de las Americas. There was another late equaliser from Lineker in the Semi Finals, as England drew 1-1 with West Germany, after extra time, before losing on penalties. Despite a subsequent 2-1 defeat against Italy in the Third Place Match, the England team emerged from the tournament with a great reputation. Fourth place was England's best placing in the World Cup since the trophy was won in 1966. On a personal level, Lineker's four goals in the tournament, added to those scored in Mexico, enabled him to join the select band of players who have scored ten or more goals in the World Cup finals.

Gary was joined at the World Cup finals by his wife, who worked for ITV during the tournament, and interviewed Roger Milla ahead of England's match against Cameroon. Michelle's role was a surprise, with footballers' wives having much less of a profile back in 1990 than they have nowadays. It also led to an unexpected encounter with Paul Gascoigne, who recounted the incident: "One of the running jokes of the 1990 World Cup centred on David Platt. He was for ever going on about Doug Ellis, the chairman of Villa, who had this brilliant boat, or so Platty was always telling us, boasting about how he had been on it. So whenever we saw some scruffy old boat, we'd all shout to Platty, 'Hey Platty, that must be Doug Ellis's'! We went to the seaside one day off in Sardinia, and Chris Waddle, John Barnes, and I went for a swim. About 300 yards out we came upon this big yacht. I said 'I bet that's Doug Ellis's'. And it was. We were invited on board and, with the help of other guests, got through about twenty bottles of his champagne. Several visitors arrived that afternoon, including Nigel Kennedy, who played his violin. There was a pop star as well, who played the piano, but I can't remember his name. Gary Lineker and his wife, Michelle, were there. She was standing sipping her champagne in the sun when I decided to leap on her as a friendly gesture. I landed on her back and we both went overboard. Gary was in a state of shock, seeing his wife disappear over the side of the yacht. But we were fine, though I admit we had a bit of a struggle getting back on board".

The following year saw Lineker score twice as Cameroon were beaten 2-0 in a Wembley friendly, and four times as Malaysia were beaten 4-2 in Kuala Lumpur – a repeat of the performance against Spain in 1987. Tottenham Hotspur won the FA Cup in 1991, beating Nottingham Forest 2-1 in the Final, after extra time, despite losing Gascoigne with an injury that was to put his career on hold for a year, while Lineker had a penalty saved. Prior to this, Lineker scored twice as Arsenal were beaten 3-1 in the Semi Finals. Gary and Michelle became parents for the first time in 1991, with the birth of their son George. As a baby, George was diagnosed as suffering from leukaemia, which was successfully treated. Both Gary and Michelle worked actively for the Leukaemia Busters charity, raising both awareness of leukaemia, and money to help treatment of the disease.

The birth of George was followed by that of three other sons for the Linekers, namely Harry (1993), Tobias (1996), and Angus (1997).

As he approached the twilight of his career, Lineker sought a new horizon, arranging a move to Nagoya Grampus Eight, a Japanese club, while announcing that he would retire from international football after the 1992 European Championship finals. During the 1991-92 season, Lineker's goals helped Spurs to reach the Quarter Finals of the European Cup-Winners' Cup. He played his final game in English domestic football as Tottenham lost 3-1 to Manchester United in May 1992. Lineker scored for Tottenham, and his goal brought a great ovation from the Old Trafford crowd.

Lineker scored England's first and last goals of the qualifying campaign for the 1992 European Championship, both of them against Poland. A late goal in Poznan gave England the 1-1 draw that secured qualification. The Euro '92 finals proved to be an anti-climatic end to Lineker's international career. After goalless draws with Denmark and France, a 2-1 defeat against Sweden brought England's elimination. Lineker was substituted during the latter stages of the match against Sweden, with this being a strange decision from Graham Taylor, given the frequency with which the player had scored vital goals for his country. Lineker unfortunately failed to score in any of his last six matches for England, including a friendly against Brazil at Wembley shortly before the Euro '92 finals, in which he missed a penalty with a scuffed shot. Lineker had played 80 times for England, and scored 48 goals, just one less than the national goalscoring record of Bobby Charlton. Lineker's achievement for England had been summed up a couple of years earlier by Bobby Robson: "He loves to score goals. He will hunt and he is brave. He will get in amongst the biggest dirtiest defenders in a bid to score a goal. I have seen him hammered to the floor time after time and he still gets up and gets on with the game. He never whinges and never tries to get anyone sent off. In terms of movement off the ball, timing his runs, making team-mates play the ball into space so that defenders have to turn, he is the best there is. He will go for anything in the box, never thinking about the challenge only the ball. He is up there with Greaves, Law, Best, Rush, Francis who all possessed electric pace which gave them that extra yard".

During 1992, the year of his move from to Japan, the high esteem in which Gary was held in Britain was marked with a series of disparate recognitions. He was awarded an OBE in the New Year's Honours List, for services to football. A few months later, he won the

Footballer of the Year award, for the second time in his career. Gary has long been a keen amateur cricketer, and he made a guest appearance for the Marylebone Cricket Club against Germany, at Lord's, in July. The match was drawn, and Lineker was dismissed having scored a single run. As he made his way back to the pavilion, he joked to spectators that "I always score one against Germany". November brought the award of the Freedom of Leicester from Leicester City Council. Lineker's spell with Nagoya Grampus Eight was frustrating, as a persistent toe injury limited him to 23 league appearances across two years, during which he scored nine goals. The injury forced Gary to retire in 1994, at the age of thirty three. Although he spent little time on the pitch, Lineker enjoyed life in Japan, being enthusiastic about the way in which he and his family were able to experience a different culture to that in Britain. He also learned to speak Japanese.

During the latter part of his playing career, Lineker, who was noted for his positive dealings with both the public and the media, thought ahead to possible new career in television. He already had a good profile in the media, having done occasional football punditry for the BBC. Lineker's exploits led to several references in the *Roy of the Rovers* comic, with a 1990 story included Gary joining Reg Race in releasing a record, with the song *Europe United* being described as "hot rocking heavy metal rap". The comedy drama *An Evening with Gary Lineker*, set against the background of the 1990 World Cup finals, written by Arthur Smith and Chris England, enjoyed a successful run in the West End from 1991 to 1993, and Gary appeared in an ITV production, which was shown on television in 1994.

Following his return from Japan, Gary built a successful career with the BBC, working on both radio and television coverage of football, and becoming the main presenter of *Match of the Day* in 1999. After a rather wooden start, Lineker's presentation of football on the BBC has grown in confidence, while his corny jokes and puns have added a new dimension. Lineker also featured on *They Think It's All Over*, the comedy sports quiz, from 1995 to 2003. Lineker patiently accepted a lot of ribbing from fellow-panellists about his toe injury, alleged goal-hanging, and large ears. Over on ITV, Lineker appeared in a series of adverts for Walker's Crisps, in which he played a bad guy who stole crisps from children – in counterpoint to his usual nice guy image. Walkers were based in Leicester, and became sponsors of Leicester City, whose Walkers Stadium (replacing Filbert Street) was opened by

Lineker in 2002. The following year Gary led a consortium which bought Leicester City, rescuing a club that had been threatened with bankruptcy. Lineker's clean image took a blow in 2006, as he and Michelle were divorced. Michelle's submission to the court spoke of Gary causing her "stress and anxiety". Three years later, Gary again demonstrated his ability to score, as he married Danielle Bux, a lingerie model from Wales, 18 years younger than himself.

10 Eric Cantona: French Ambassador

"1966 was a good year for English football. Eric was born". The slogan comes from a poster advert for Nike, featuring Eric Cantona. The irony was perfectly fitting, as Cantona was a Frenchman who illuminated English football. Indeed Cantona exerted a massive influence on the domestic game in England, winning the domestic championship with both Leeds United and Manchester United, in contrast to a mixed career in his native land. Cantona played the game in the manner of a wayward genius, who apparently saw himself as the football equivalent of Arthur Rimbaud, the French poet. In more prosaic terms, Cantona can be described as an attacking midfielder, with great vision and passing ability, and a high goalscoring ratio.

Cantona was born on May 24 1966, in Paris, but grew up in his family's home at Caillols, in Marseille. The Cantona family had originated from Sardinia before moving to France. Cantona's maternal ancestry was Spanish, including a grandfather, Pedro Raurich, who had fought for the Republicans in the Spanish Civil War, before taking exile in France, during the dictatorship of General Franco. In his autobiography, published in 1994, Cantona would note that he was born shortly before England won the World Cup, and that elsewhere during 1966 Isabelle, his future wife was "somewhere in the streets of Orange", while the Beatles' record *Paperback Writer* was a worldwide hit.

Eric had a happy childhood, and took to playing football from an early age, supporting Marseille. In his book Cantona recalled attending a European Cup match in October 1971 between Marseille and Ajax – the boy, aged 5, watched while perched on his father's shoulders. Ajax won the match 2-1, and went on to win the competition that season – this being the second in their hat trick of European titles. Cantona's imagination was captured by the Netherlands team in the 1974 World Cup, and he lamented the victory of West Germany in the Final as "a dark betrayal of the beautiful play of the Dutch". Eric joined the Caillols youth team, and featured in their 3-0 win over Vitrolles in the Final of the Cup of Provence in 1978. Three years later, at the age of 15, Cantona joined Auxerre, a club in the French first division.

Cantona made rapid progress through Auxerre's junior and reserve teams, and in 1982 made his debut for France's Youth team. Cantona's debut for the Auxerre first team followed in October 1983, when he was aged 17. The requirement to do national service for a year, from turning 18, put Cantona's football career on hold. On the other hand, he enjoyed playing for the French Army's football team, at various foreign locations, and a trip to Gabon made a big impression on the young man. Thereafter Cantona's career in French domestic football was characterised by rapid moves between a series of clubs, and recurring disciplinary problems. Cantona was loaned to Martigues in 1985, and returned to Auxerre the following year, at which point he signed his first professional contract. Cantona established himself as an excellent player for Auxerre, but also started to show a fiery temperament. Away from the football pitch, he enjoyed a romance with Isabelle Ferrer, whose brother, Bernard, was a team-mate of Eric's at Auxerre. Eric and Isabelle married in 1987, and were to have two children, Raphael, born in 1988, and Josephine, born 1995.

Cantona soon gained a place in the national squad, making his debut for France against West Germany in August 1987, at the age of 21. Cantona scored in this match, but France lost 2-1. Cantona also featured in France's Under-21 team, which won the European Championship for this age range in 1988, beating England 6-4 on aggregate in the Semi Finals, and Greece 3-0 on aggregate in the Final. In September 1988 Cantona was banned from the national team for insulting the coach, Henri Michel, in a television interview. Henri Michel was sacked as coach of France a few weeks later, and replaced by Michel Platini. Cantona was recalled to the national team by Platini, and featured in the 1990 World Cup qualifiers, but France failed to the make the finals, finishing behind Yugoslavia and Scotland.

In the Summer of 1988, Cantona moved from Auxerre to Marseille, for a French record fee, after rejecting a possible move to Milan. He did not immediately fit in at Marseille, and this led to Cantona being lent to Bordeaux for latter part of 1988-89 season – thereby missing out on participation in Marseille winning the French League and Cup double. Cantona was loaned to Montpellier for the whole of the 1989-90 season, which culminated in the club winning the French Cup, and he played in the 2-1 victory over Racing Club de France in the Final. Cantona returned to Marseille for the 1990-91 season, at the end of which the club won the League, but Cantona again did not settle at the club, as he had difficult relations with Raymond Goethals, the coach, and Bernard Tapie, the owner. Cantona only played in 18 of Marseille's 38 league matches that season. Marseille finished as runners-up in the European Cup at the end of the season, losing to Red Star Belgrade on penalties after a dreadful goalless draw, but

Cantona, who had played in earlier games in the campaign, did not feature in the Final. Marseille now dispensed with Cantona, and he moved to Nimes. Within a few months of the move, Cantona's ill-discipline surfaced again. In December 1991 Cantona threw the ball at a referee, who had made a decision the player disagreed with. A hearing at the French Football Federation banned Cantona for a month, whereupon he called the members of the disciplinary panel idiots. The ban was increased to three months, and a frustrated Cantona announced he had decided to retire from football – he was aged 25 at the time.

Michel Platini persuaded Cantona to reconsider his decision. Seeking a new start, Cantona travelled to England at the beginning of 1992. He appeared set to join Sheffield Wednesday, having attracted the attention of their manager, Trevor Francis, but the proposed deal broke down, with Cantona refusing to undergo a trial period with the club – Cantona felt his standing as an international player was sufficient proof of ability. Cantona looked elsewhere, and signed for Leeds United at the start of February. He also played for France in a 2-0 defeat against England, at Wembley, that month. During the remainder of the 1991-92 season, Cantona helped Leeds win the League title, for the first time since 1974, finishing ahead of runners-up Manchester United. The supporters at Leeds lauded Cantona, and began the chant "Ooh, aah, Cantona!" that followed him for the remainder of his career. During the Summer, Cantona played for France in the Euro '92 finals. France had won all eight of their matches in the qualifiers, with Cantona scoring in victories against Iceland which opened and closed the campaign. Cantona appeared in each of France's matches in the finals, but draws with Sweden and England, followed by a defeat against Denmark (described by Cantona as "a happy and unexpected team which was to go on to take the title") meant the French were eliminated at the group stage. This proved to be Cantona's only participation in a major international tournament. Platini resigned as coach of France following the tournament, and was replaced by Gerard Houllier.

There was a brighter outcome at the start of the new domestic season in England, as in August 1992 Cantona scored a hat trick when Leeds United beat Liverpool 4-3 in the Charity Shield, at Wembley. The previous season's League title took Leeds into the European Cup, but they appeared to have thrown away their opening tie against Stuttgart by losing 3-0 in Germany. A 4-1 win by Leeds in the return, including a goal from Cantona, levelled the aggregate score, but they had been defeated on away goals. Stuttgart, however, had fielded four foreign players, exceeding the competition limit of three such players per match. In the surprising absence of any provision in the European Cup's rules to deal with such an infringement, UEFA considered the matter for a few days, before awarding the second leg to Leeds 3-0, and ordering that the tie be settled by a play-off at a neutral venue. Leeds completed their great escape by beating Stuttgart 2-1 at Barcelona's Nou Camp stadium, before only 7,000 spectators. In the next round Leeds were eliminated by Rangers, with the Scottish champions winning both legs 2-1 – Cantona scored for Leeds in the second match.

Cantona rapidly become unsettled at Leeds United, just as he had at French clubs in the past. When Manchester United's manager, Alex Ferguson, made a speculative enquiry about Cantona's availability, Leeds United quickly accepted a £1,200,000 bid for the player. Less than ten months after arriving at Leeds, Cantona hopped across the Pennines, joining Manchester United on November 26 1992. Cantona rapidly became a star of the United team, which went on to win the Premier League in its inaugural 1992-93 season. United's triumph was secured by winning their last seven matches of the Premier League campaign, to eventually finish 10 points clear of runners-up Aston Villa. This sequence started with a 3-1 victory against Norwich City, who were at that time contending for the title – Cantona scored in this game. A few weeks later the trophy was secured, and Cantona had won the English title with two different clubs in successive seasons.

Cantona's arrival at Manchester United inspired a poetry competition in the club's magazine. The player proudly featured two of the poems in his autobiography, including this paean written by a female supporter:

Some see you from a distance, admire you from afar
To them you're just that Frenchman, that Eric Cantona
I wish I could be like them, admiring only skill
Instead of wanting more than just magnificent goalmouth thrills
Your intelligence alarms me, so rare in such a trade
Your sultry gaze unnerves me, it could easily persuade
Should you ever be in need, *cher*, of company at the bar
Please let me bring new meaning to that famous chant "Ooh, ah"!

At start of 1993-94 season, United won the Charity Shield, beating Arsenal on penalties, following a 1-1 draw. United began a European Cup campaign with a 5-3 aggregate win against Kispest Honved, with Cantona among the scorers. In the next round, United built up a two goal lead against Galatasaray in the first quarter of an hour at Old Trafford, before the Turks came back strongly, and the home side needed a late goal from Cantona to escape with a 3-3 draw. A bruising goalless draw in the second leg took the Galatasaray through on away goals. After the final whistle, Cantona made a sarcastic gesture to Kurt Rothlisberger, the Swiss referee, which earned him a red card. Both Cantona and Bryan Robson were then attacked by Turkish policemen during a skirmish in the players' tunnel. Elsewhere during the Autumn of 1993, France were unexpectedly eliminated in the 1994 World Cup qualifiers. France lost 3-2 at home to Israel in their penultimate game, with Israel (who finished bottom of the group) scoring twice in the last five minutes. France then lost 2-1 at home to Bulgaria, who scored the winner in the final minute. These results left France a point short of qualifying. Cantona, who had opened the scoring against Bulgaria, was very disappointed with the team's failure to reach the World Cup finals. Houllier now resigned as the coach, and his replacement, Aime Jacquet, appointed Cantona as captain of the national team.

Manchester United won the League and FA Cup double in the Spring of 1994, for the first time in the club's history. Cantona scored 18 times in the Premiership this season, but was sent off in successive games against Swindon Town and Arsenal during the latter part of the season. Cantona scored twice from the penalty spot in the 4-0 win against Chelsea in the FA Cup Final. Ahead of the first of these penalties, Chelsea's Dennis Wise attempted to distract Cantona by offering a £100 bet that he would fail to score. United had also hoped to win the League Cup, but they lost 3-1 to Aston Villa in the Final. Cantona's contribution to United's success this season led to his winning the Professional Footballers' Association Player of the Year award for 1994.

In 1994 Cantona published *My Story*, an autobiography. Cantona provided a fascinating account of his life, setting the football career in a wide context, with inspiration being gained from both sporting heroes and cultural figures. The book's Preface opened with Cantona stating "I have always had idols, people I have admired and who I still admire. In music, football, writing and elsewhere. People who have meant something to me. Also small phrases, little words, taken here and there at the whim of my mood". This was rapidly followed by references to Jim Morrison, Arthur Rimbaud, Leo Ferre, Marlon Brando, and Mickey Rourke. The wonderful imagery in the following passage from Cantona is far removed from the bland statements that characterise most football memoirs: "An artist, in my eyes, is someone who can lighten up a dark room. I have never and will never find any difference between the pass from Pele to Carlos Alberto in the final of the World Cup in 1970 in Mexico and the poetry of the young Rimbaud, who stretches 'cords from steeple to steeple and garlands from window to window'. There is in each of these human manifestations an expression of beauty which touches us and gives us a feeling of eternity".

In France, Cantona's enthusiasm for art, and volatile temperament, led to his being lampooned in the television programme *Guignols de l'Info*, an equivalent of the British *Spitting Image*. Cantona's puppet character in the French programme was called "Picasso". In his book, Cantona commented favourably on this humorous portrayal of his personality. The character "Picasso" frequently swore on the programme, and once painted a red card which he showed to himself. Within a few months of the appearance of his autobiography, a red card in the real world led to a disciplinary crisis for Cantona, which was more serious than those of the past.

Manchester United retained the Charity Shield at the start of the 1994-95 season, with Cantona scoring in the 2-0 victory against Blackburn Rovers. Following this Manchester United became the first English club to feature in the group stage of the European Cup / Champions League, having been given automatic qualification as one of the top seeds. Cantona was suspended from the first four of United's six group matches, as a result of his sending off against Galatasaray the previous season, and the team were eliminated, finishing behind Gothenburg and Barcelona. In domestic football, the season started to unravel for United on January 25 1995, the date on which Cantona was sent off in a Premiership game against Crystal Palace. As he left the field, Cantona lashed out with a Kung-fu kick on a Palace supporter who had been abusing the player from the stands. Amidst general outrage at Cantona's action, he was suspended for the remainder of the season by United, and this ban was extended to the end of September 1995 by the Football Association. Graham Kelly, Chief Executive of the FA, described Cantona's action as "a stain on our game". Criminal proceedings against Cantona led to his being

84

sentenced to fourteen days in prison for assault, but this was reduced on appeal to a requirement that Cantona perform community service. In the aftermath of the incident, Cantona famously told a press conference that "When the seagulls follow the trawler, it's because they think sardines will be thrown in to the sea". It appeared that Cantona was comparing the journalists who frequently followed him, seeking scraps of information, with the actions of seagulls. United lost form without Cantona, and finished second in the Premiership, behind Blackburn Rovers, with this being the only season they did not win the title while Cantona was at the club. United also finished as runners-up in the FA Cup, losing 1-0 to Everton in the Final.

Cantona returned from suspension in October 1995, and scored in his first match back in the United team, a 2-2 draw with Liverpool. During the closing stages of the 1995-96 season, Cantona scored several important goals as Manchester United overhauled Newcastle United to win the Premiership title, and he ended the season with 14 league goals. Having trailed by 12 points in January, United eventually finished four points ahead of Newcastle. Cantona scored the only goal as Manchester United beat Newcastle at the start of March, with this being the first of six successive Premiership games in which he scored – with four of these games being 1-0 victories. The season ended with another vital goal from Cantona, by which Manchester United beat Liverpool 1-0 in the FA Cup Final. Cantona scored with a spectacular shot five minutes from time, and became the first player from outside the British Isles to captain the winning team in a FA Cup Final. United had now won the league and FA Cup double for the second time in three seasons. Cantona also won the Footballer of the Year award this season.

A few weeks later the Euro 96 finals were staged in England, but Cantona was not included in France's squad. Cantona had led the French team in the early part of the Euro 96 qualifiers, but was stripped of the national captaincy, and removed from the team, during the English ban in 1995. Cantona's great form for Manchester United during the 1995-96 season prompted suggestions of a recall, but Aime Jacquet decided to keep faith with the players who had completed the Euro 96 qualifiers, rather than possibly unsettling the French team with a recall for Cantona. The suspension of Cantona during 1995 effectively ended an international career in which he had played 45 times for France, scoring 20 goals.

In August 1996 Cantona scored as Manchester United beat Newcastle United 4-0 in the Charity Shield. Manchester United returned to the Champions League in 1996-97, and became the first English team to advance from the league stage of the competition. In the Quarter Finals, an inspired United beat Porto 4-0 at Old Trafford, producing one of their best ever European performances, with Cantona among the goalscorers. The return was leg was a goalless draw. Manchester United's run came to an end in the Semi Finals, as they lost both legs 1-0 to Borussia Dortmund. The second leg proved to be Cantona's final European match. In contrast to his brilliance in domestic football, Cantona had been relatively ineffective in Europe across several seasons. At the end of the season Manchester United retained their Premiership title, finishing seven points clear of three other clubs – Newcastle United, Arsenal, and Liverpool. Earlier in the season, during October 1996, Manchester United had been thrashed 5-0 by Newcastle United, and lost 6-3 to Southampton in their next match. November started with Manchester United losing 2-1 against Chelsea, but the three consecutive defeats were followed by a run in which United won eleven, and drew five, of their next sixteen Premiership matches. Cantona scored 11 Premiership goals this season, appearing in thirty six of Manchester United's thirty eight matches, including the final game of the campaign, this being a 2-0 win against West Ham United on May 11. Seven days later, Cantona unexpectedly announced his retirement from football, aged only 30.

Unlike the impetuous announcement in France in 1991, this time Cantona was fully resolved on retirement, although the reason for the decision was not clear at the time. Cantona subsequently explained that his retirement stemmed from disillusionment with the growing influence of commercialism at Manchester United. In an interview with *L'Equipe* in 2007, to mark the tenth anniversary of the retirement, Cantona said: "I did not have the flame any more. Football was my life, my childhood passion. When the flame disappears, why continue? To go to the Middle East for €300 billion? I was not interested in that". Cantona reflected that he might have continued playing football if he had a chance to play for France, the host nation, in the 1998 World Cup finals, or if United had won the Champions League.

Cantona moved away from England, living in Barcelona for the next three years, before returning to France. Within a few months of leaving the professional game, Cantona became involved in beach football, and played for the France's national team in this new variant of the sport. Cantona subsequently managed France as they won the inaugural FIFA Beach Soccer World Cup in 2005, and scored in a 7-4 victory against Spain in the Quarter Finals. He remained the manager of France through the next three Beach Soccer World Cups, as they took third place in 2006, and fourth place in 2007, before being eliminated in the Quarter Finals of the 2008 tournament, for which France were the hosts. Cantona found another football role in 2011, becoming Director of Soccer at the reformed New York Cosmos.

In an unusual turn for a footballer, Cantona has established himself in a career in cinema, primarily as an actor, while having additional roles as a director and producer. He has featured in a series of French films from 1995 onwards. In his best-known film, Cantona played a French ambassador to England in *Elizabeth*, a 1998 British dramatisation of part of the reign of Queen Elizabeth I. Eric began a relationship with Rachida Brakni, an actress he met when they worked together on the French film *L'Outremangeur*, released in 2003. This led to Eric being divorced from his wife Isabelle, following which he married Rachida in 2007. Moving from the large screen to the small screen, Cantona has appeared in television advertisements, most notably playing football in a various settings to promote Nike. Cantona assumed the role of a King of England in an advert by betting company Partouche, which coincided with the Euro 2008 finals. In January 2012 it appeared Cantona intended to seek nomination as a candidate in the French Presidential election, but this proved to be a publicity stunt, aimed at drawing attention to a campaign on housing issues.

Eric Cantona has remained a fascinating figure on the fringes of English football. He abruptly ended ties with Manchester United in 1997, but remained interested in the progress of the club. He returned to Old Trafford in 1998 for a match that raised money for the survivors of the Munich air crash, and the families of the United players killed in that disaster. United won 8-4 against an Invitation XI, selected by Cantona, who played the first half for his impromptu team, and the second half for United. In 2002 Cantona was among the players inducted into the newly-established English Football Hall of Fame, being the only non-British player among this group. Three years later, Manchester United were bought by the Glazer family from the USA, a development which prompted critical comments from Cantona. There has been intermittent speculation that Cantona will eventually return to Manchester United in a coaching role. Cantona fuelled this during an interview with Italian newspaper *Gazzetta dello Sport* in 2009, stating that he would like to coach either Manchester United or England. On an immediate level, 2009 brought the release of *Looking for Eric*, a British film in which Cantona played himself. The film revolves around an English postman, the character being named Eric Bishop, who idolises Cantona, and receives guidance from his hero. At one point Bishop says to Cantona "Sometimes we forget you're just a man". Cantona's response is to announce "I am not a man, I am Cantona", with a mock-stern expression that dissolves into a smile.

11 David Beckham: Cultural Icon

David Beckham is one of the world's most famous footballers, but his high profile does not just stem from his achievements on the pitch. Beckham starred for the Manchester United team which dominated the English domestic game around the turn of the Millennium, before moving to Real Madrid, and then LA Galaxy. He was a regular member of the national team for over a decade, but Beckham's displays for his country were often embroiled in controversy. The player has made as many headlines off the pitch as on the pitch, with these often emanating from his celebrity marriage to Victoria Adams.

Beckham was born on May 2 1975, at Leytonstone in London. The son of Ted Beckham, a keen amateur player, David became obsessed with football as a child, with many hours of practice. In December 1986, at the age of eleven, Beckham won a Bobby Charlton Soccer Skills competition, this being part of the coaching of youngsters organised by the former Manchester United player. Beckham, who was a United fan, received his award at Old Trafford. Beckham was given a trial by Manchester United in 1988, and signed with the club as a schoolboy the following year, when aged fourteen. Having become an apprentice in July 1991, Beckham was part of the team which won the FA Youth Cup in 1992. The line-up included Nicky Butt, Simon Davies, Keith Gillespie, Gary Neville, and Ryan Giggs, each of whom would star for United's first team, and play international football.

Beckham made his first team debut as a substitute against Brighton and Hove Albion, in a League Cup match in September 1992. He signed as a professional in January 1993, but did not make any further appearances in the Manchester United first team until the 1994-95 season. He scored his first professional goal in December 1994, as Galatasaray were beaten 4-0 in the European Cup. During the Spring of 1995 United loaned Beckham to Preston North End, a Third Division club, to enable him to get extra first team experience, but the player was soon recalled to United, and made his first four appearances in the Premiership at the end of the season. Beckham became a regular in the Manchester United first team during 1995-96. At the end of the season, United won the Premiership and FA Cup double, with Beckham (who had just turned twenty one) playing in the 1-0 win against Liverpool in the FA Cup Final. Beckham's progress owed much to Alex Ferguson, manager of United since 1986, who had revived the youth policy established decades earlier by Matt Busby, and was a great mentor to the youngsters who reached the first team.

On the opening day of the 1996-97 season, Beckham scored an amazing goal as United beat Wimbledon 3-0. Seeing that Neil Sullivan, the Wimbledon goalkeeper, had ventured forward, Beckham beat him with a lofted shot from the halfway line – later measured at 57 yards. Beckham and United continued to flourish this season, and retained the Premiership title. By contrast, in 1997-98 Arsenal won the double, with United taking second place in the Premiership. Playing on the right-hand side of midfield, Beckham set up many goals with his excellent crossing and passing. He was also brilliant taker of free kicks, scoring spectacular goals. As his play matured, Beckham became equally adept as a central midfielder. Besides replacing Eric Cantona as a focal point in the Manchester United team, Beckham became a mainstay of the England team. Off the field, Beckham began a relationship with Victoria Adams, better known as Posh Spice, from the Spice Girls. This coupling of two celebrities, nicknamed "Posh and Becks", drew increasing media interest, which was fuelled by their engagement at the start of 1998.

Beckham made his England debut in September 1996, as Moldova were beaten 3-0 in a World Cup qualifier. He went on to play in all eight of England's qualifying matches, but was omitted from the team by Glenn Hoddle, the coach, as England beat Tunisia 2-0 in their first match of the finals, held in France in 1998. Hoddle later wrote, in his infamous book *My 1998 World Cup Story*, that Beckham "wasn't as focused and sharp as he might have been in our warm-up games" Hoddle added: "There had been a vagueness about him, on and off the pitch, and sometimes in training. I'm sure he was missing Victoria, who's away a great deal". Beckham appeared as a substitute in the next match, but England lost 2-1 to Romania. Hoddle put Beckham in the starting line-up against Colombia, and the player scored his first international goal, with a brilliant free kick, as England won 2-0. Beckham's World Cup came to an abrupt halt in the next match, as he was sent off for retaliating when provoked by Argentina's Diego Simeone. The match was drawn 2-2, following which Argentina won on penalties. Beckham's silly act, which forced England to play almost all of the second half, plus extra time, a man short, severely limited the team's attacking options, and was widely regarded as the cause of the team's elimination.

Beckham was vilified by many in England, and abused by the supporters of teams that United played the following season. Beckham refused to be provoked, and concentrated on his game. Indeed the 1998-99 season proved to be the high point of Beckham's career with United, as the club achieved a unique treble, winning the Premiership, FA Cup, and Champions League. The Premiership title was secured with a 2-1 win against Tottenham Hotspur, in which Beckham scored, following which Newcastle United were beaten 2-0 in the FA Cup Final. In the Champions League Final, United trailed against Bayern Munich for almost the entire match. Beckham later recalled his thoughts shortly before the end of normal time: "When I looked up and saw the big clock showing one minute I was convinced that was it. I don't remember much apart from how gutted I was feeling. It was one of the worst moments I had experienced on a football pitch. I even saw the trophy up in the stands with Bayern Munich ribbons already on it. It was an unbelievable sight. I was almost sick". United bounced back with a couple of goals during stoppage time, each following a corner from Beckham, to grab a sensational 2-1 victory.

David and Victoria were married on July 4 1999, at Luttrellstown Castle, in Ireland. A quiet wedding ceremony, attended by a small group of family and friends, was followed by a lavish reception – rumours suggested it cost £500,000 – in the grounds of the castle. Amidst tight security, the Beckhams sold exclusive rights to pictures of the wedding to *OK* magazine for a reported £1,000,000 fee. Their first son Brooklyn, named after the place where he was conceived when David joined Victoria in the USA immediately after the World Cup finals, had been born on March 4 1999. The extravagance, and celebrity lifestyle, of the Beckhams started to raise questions among the football community. Their opulent home in Hertfordshire was derided as Beckingham Palace. David was emerging as one of the most recognisable figures in advertising, as he endorsed a variety of products. He secured major deals with Adidas, Brylcreem, and Pepsi, and used his first payment from Adidas to buy a Porsche for £85,000. Beckham also became a fashion icon, wearing some unexpected clothes, chosen for him by Victoria.

At the end of 1999 Manchester United's treble became a quadruple, as Beckham helped them beat Palmeiras 1-0, in Tokyo, to become the first British team to win the World Club Championship. Participation in the inaugural FIFA Club World Championship, held in Brazil during January 2000, was not a success. Beckham was sent off as

United drew 1-1 with Necaxa in their first match, and the team failed to progress beyond the group stage. Although sometimes embarrassed by his wife's pronouncements, Beckham was a devoted family man. In February 2000 he missed a training session at United in order to look after Brooklyn, who was unwell – and was dropped by Alex Ferguson from the team's match against Leeds United a few days later. At the end of the 1999-2000 season United retained the Premiership title, with an eighteen point margin over runners-up Arsenal.

In the Summer Beckham played for England in the Euro 2000 finals. He had been a regular member of the team during a troubled qualifying campaign, which had seen Glenn Hoddle resign, and be replaced – initially on a temporary basis – by Kevin Keegan. England stormed to an early 2-0 lead against Portugal in their first match of the finals, but then fell apart, and lost 3-2. As the players left the field at the end of the match, Beckham directed an angry gesture towards England fans who had been barracking him. England recovered to beat Germany 1-0 in their next game, with Alan Shearer heading in a free kick from Beckham. A 3-2 defeat against Romania brought England's elimination at the end of the group stage.

Massive public interest in David Beckham led Staffordshire University to announce in March 2000 that they were organising a course in football studies, with Beckham as a major focus. This would act as a module within a variety of degree courses. Professor Ellis Cashmole explained: "We'll be examining the rise of football from its folk origins in the 17th century, to the power it's become and the central place it occupies in British culture, and indeed world culture, today. We do have to concede that Beckham occupies a lot of our attention today. He's the object of a great many fantasies, and he and his wife seem to mesmerise the population, so we will be looking at the reasons why this has come about. He married very well, and he's a good-looking guy, and he's gifted with a fair degree of technical skills. I think he embodies the spirit of the times, he doesn't actually say much or do much – unlike icons of the past, he doesn't take a political stand or engage with any kind of social issues of the day. But maybe that's just we want in the early 21st century, a person who doesn't actually do much, but onto which we can displace all our fantasies. He occupies so much of our attention, we write and we talk about him. He is a central figure in our culture at the moment, like him or loathe him".

Beckham added to the interest in him with the publication of an autobiography, *My World*, which appeared in October 2000, with an updated version the following year. The front cover featured a lurid and red-tinted picture of Beckham, with this hair cropped – every inch the Red Devil. Equal coverage was given to the text, written by Beckham with a couple of assistants, and the photos from Dean Freeman, commissioned specifically for the book. The text was unusually revealing for a footballer, with many honest and brave revelations. Beckham recalls the abuse he received after the 1998 World Cup finals, saying: "The manager [Alex Ferguson] told me to ignore all the criticism that was coming my way but I did take note of some of the people who slaughtered me after Argentina. I've got a little book in which I've written down the names of those people who upset me the most. I don't want to name them because I want it to be a surprise when I get them back. I know I will get them some day".

England's qualifying campaign for the 2002 World Cup opened in October 2000 with a 1-0 defeat against Germany. Beckham was England's best player on the day, leading a second half rally after the team made a poor start to the match. The defeat prompted Keegan to resign as manager. Beckham captained England for the first time during the following month, being selected for the role by the caretaker manager, Peter Taylor, as England lost 1-0 to Italy. Sven-Goran Eriksson took over as manager during the early part of 2001, and retained Beckham as England captain. The World Cup qualifying campaign ended in October 2001, with a 2-2 draw against Greece at Old Trafford, by which England secured a place in the finals. Having led a fight-back with a determined personal display, Beckham gained the vital point for England by scoring a brilliant goal with a thirty yard free kick in stoppage time. This performance went a long way towards securing Beckham the BBC Sports Personality of the Year award at the end of 2001.

United won the Premiership title for a third successive season in 2000-01, finishing ten points clear of Arsenal. During the Spring of 2002, Beckham suffered a broken metatarsal, playing for United against Deportivo La Coruna, in the Quarter Finals of the Champions League. He missed the remainder of United's season, and the club failed to win any trophies, finishing third in the Premiership, and losing on away goals to Bayer Leverkusen in the Champions League Semi Finals. Prior to his injury, Beckham had been in great form, scoring a personal best total of 11 Premiership goals this season.

Beckham managed to recover sufficiently to join the England squad for the World Cup finals, held in Japan and South Korea. England began with a 1-1 draw against Sweden, in which a tiring Beckham was substituted midway through the second half. The next match saw England beat Argentina, with Beckham scoring the only goal from a penalty, thereby exorcising demons from the 1998 match. Unfortunately the continuing effects of his injury hampered Beckham during the remainder of the finals. After drawing 0-0 with Nigeria, and beating Denmark 3-0, England exited with a tame performance against Brazil, who won the Quarter Final meeting 2-1. Despite some lacklustre performances on the pitch, the impression was that Beckham was one of the stars of the World Cup, as he received great adulation from the local public. He was already an established celebrity in the region due to advertising work.

Romeo, the second son of David and Victoria, was born on September 1 2002. During the following months speculation mounted that Beckham would be sold by United, due to a rift with Alex Ferguson, who was tired of Beckham's celebrity lifestyle, seeing it as a distraction from his playing career. The Beckhams' thirst for celebrity appeared to be led by Victoria, whose attempts to establish a solo singing career, following the split of the Spice Girls, had floundered. When United were eliminated from the FA Cup by Arsenal in February 2003, a dressing room row saw Ferguson hurl a football boot at Beckham, causing the player an injury. United's Champions League campaign ended with elimination by Real Madrid in the Quarter Finals, as the Spanish club won the tie 6-5 on aggregate – Beckham was reduced to a substitute role in the second leg, but scored twice when he joined the fray. This contact with Real Madrid led Beckham to conclude that he would like to join the club. The 2002-03 season closed with United winning the Premiership, finishing fifteen points clear of Arsenal. This was the sixth time that Beckham was part of a title-winning team.

In June 2003 the award of an OBE to Beckham was announced in the Queen's Birthday Honours – upon the recommendation of Tony Blair. Five years after the sending off against Argentina, Beckham's transformation into a football role model was complete. The award was rapidly followed by the much-predicted sale of Beckham by Manchester United. He moved to Real Madrid, for a transfer fee that was expected to total £24,500,000 once all of the instalments had been paid. Beckham immediately joined Real on tour of the Far East, where the club capitalised upon the merchandising profile of their new star. Indeed David and Victoria had recently toured the region as a couple, apparently earning millions by advertising beauty products.

Beckham published *My Side*, a more conventional autobiography than *My World*, in September 2003. The new book rapidly became one of Britain's best ever selling football books, with sales of 100,000 copies in the first week. In a repeat of the dual release of *My World*, the initial hardback version of *My Side* was followed by a paperback update a year later. During the early part of 2004 it appeared David's marriage to Victoria was under strain. There was speculation that Victoria was not happy with the idea of settling in Spain. The tabloid press carried lurid stories of an alleged recent relationship between David and Rebecca Loos, his personal assistant. Loos, who was openly bisexual, sold her story to the *News of the World*, and other media outlets, for a total of £700,000 with the backing of the publicist, Max Clifford – he proclaimed the story to be "the greatest tabloid expose of the past decade".

Beckham scored four goals for England in the Euro 2004 qualifiers, but missed a penalty in the 0–0 draw with Turkey that made certain of a place in the finals – losing his footing, and sending the ball high over the crossbar. Beckham's displays at the finals, in Portugal, fell well below his normal form. He missed a penalty in the 2-1 defeat against France with which England started the tournament. Victories against Switzerland and Croatia took England to the Quarter Finals, where they drew 2-2 with Portugal, after extra time. The match was settled on penalties, with Portugal winning, and Beckham being one of the England players to miss from a disintegrating penalty spot, shooting over the bar.

Over the border in Spain, Beckham had quickly established himself as one of the "galacticos" at Real Madrid, despite strong competition for places in the team. On the other hand, the club failed to live up to the reputation it had gained in winning the Champions League in 1998, 2000, and 2002. Real Madrid slumped to fourth place in the Spanish League at the end of 2003-04, Beckham's first season with the club. Although Real Madrid reached the Spanish Cup Final in 2004, and Beckham opened the scoring in the match against Real Zaragoza, his team were eventually beaten 3-2, after extra time. Real Madrid finished second in the Spanish League in both the 2004-05 and 2005-06 seasons. Real also under-performed in the Champions League, and were destined to be eliminated at the last 16 stage in each of the four season that Beckham was with the club.

Beckham's form for England in the 2006 World Cup qualifiers was indifferent. In October 2004 Beckham scored a brilliant goal for England, as they beat Wales 2-0 in a qualifying match, at Old Trafford. Beckham picked up an injury in this match, which he thought would rule him out of England's next World Cup game, a few days later. Carrying a yellow card from a previous match, Beckham now got himself booked with a rash challenge on an opponent, in order to serve a suspension for two bookings while out injured. Beckham publicly admitted the ruse, and was pilloried by many for perpetrating a cynical foul on an opponent, while being praised by others for his (rather twisted) honesty. A place in the finals was ultimately secured with a 1-0 win against Austria at Old Trafford in October 2005, but Beckham departed half an hour from time, being sent off as he received two yellow cards a minute apart. Each booking was unlucky, but Beckham's petulant behaviour contributed to the dismissal. He now set the unenviable record of becoming the first player to be sent off twice for England. He was also left to serve a second suspension in the space of a year. It appeared that family worries had unsettled Beckham, with Romeo having been rushed to hospital suffering from convulsions a few days before the match.

Off the pitch, Beckham remained active on several fronts. At the start of 2005, a year in which he reached the age of 30, Beckham became a UNICEF goodwill ambassador, building upon previous charity work. The Beckhams' third son, Cruz, was born on February 20 2005. In July of that year, London's bid to stage the 2012 Olympics was successful, with Beckham widely credited for an influential role in Singapore, where the decision was made by Olympic officials. In November 2005 Beckham opened football academies for children, which he had initiated, in both Los Angeles and London. Nearly two decades after his time with Bobby Charlton's coaching programme, Beckham was passing his experience on to the next generation. In April 2006 Beckham surprisingly announced that he was suffering from Obsessive Compulsive Disorder. In this respect, Beckham was following in the footsteps of Paul Gascoigne, a former England team-mate, who had revealed a terrible struggle with OCD, and other demons. During an interview for an ITV documentary about his life, Beckham explained "I have got this Obsessive Compulsive Disorder where I have to have everything in a straight line, or everything has to be in pairs. I'll put my Pepsi cans in the fridge and if there's one too many then I'll put it in another cupboard somewhere. I've got that problem. I'll go into a hotel room. Before I can relax I have to move all the leaflets and all the books and put them in a drawer. Everything has to be perfect".

Beckham captained the England team at the 2006 World Cup finals, staged in Germany. England's performances in the tournament were disappointing, and Beckham failed to provide the spark of leadership, although he did make some significant contributions. England beat Paraguay 1-0 in their first match, with a free kick from Beckham after three minutes leading to an own goal by Carlos Gammara. England subsequently won 2-0 against Trinidad and Tobago, and completed the group stage with a 2-2 draw against Sweden. In the Second Round, England beat Ecuador 1-0, with Beckham scoring from a free kick, but he struggled with the effects of dehydration, and vomited during the match. England's campaign ended in the Quarter Finals, with a defeat against Portugal on penalties, following a match that was drawn 0-0 after extra time. A clearly distraught Beckham had departed shortly after half time, due to an injury. The following day Beckham announced that he was resigning as England captain.

A few weeks after the World Cup finals, Beckham was excluded from the first England squad selected by new manager Steve McClaren (who had previously been part of Sven-Goran Eriksson's England coaching team, and assistant to Alex Ferguson when Beckham was at Manchester United). McClaren said he wanted to move forward with younger players in the Euro 2008 qualifiers. Beckham was unable to command a regular place in the Real Madrid first team through much of the 2006-07 season, and the club announced at the start of 2007 that his contract would not be renewed. Beckham responded by agreeing a lucrative move to Los Angeles Galaxy, which would take effect in the Summer of 2007. Beckham was reportedly expected to earn £125,000,000 during a five year deal with the club, as massive advertising and merchandising income would be paid in addition to his salary. Beckham spoke about a new challenge, but many in the game felt that he was turning his back on top-level football, in return for a Hollywood lifestyle. David and Victoria soon purchased a mansion in Beverly Hills, California, for a reputed USD 22,000,000, and this became the family's home when David moved to LA Galaxy.

Ironically the latter part of the 2006-07 season saw Beckham enjoy his best spell of form at Real Madrid, as he helped the club win the Spanish title for the first time since 2002-03 – the campaign immediately before his arrival. Beckham made clear his desire to play again for England and, after several months of speculation over a possible recall, the player was brought back into the fold by McClaren at the end of the 2006-07 season. Beckham returned as England played their first match at the new Wembley Stadium, a 1-1 draw against Brazil. A few days later Beckham gave a great display, despite struggling with an injury, as England won 3-0 away to Estonia in a Euro 2008 qualifier. England eventually failed to qualify for the Euro 2008 finals, and McClaren was sacked by the Football Association.

McClaren was replaced as England coach by Fabio Capello, who had recently managed Beckham at Real Madrid. With Beckham struggling at LA Galaxy, due to injury, he was omitted from Capello's first England squad at the start of 2008. Beckham was soon back in the national team, making his one hundredth appearance for England in a 1-0 defeat against France in March 2008. During the early part of both 2009 and 2010, Beckham had spells on loan with Milan, to coincide with close-seasons for LA Galaxy. Given a new impetus by Capello, England played excellent football in the 2010 qualifiers, winning nine of their ten matches, and scoring 34 goals. Croatia were beaten 4-1 away, with Theo Walcott scoring a hat trick, and 5-1 at home. The campaign began with eight successive victories, this being England's longest ever winning sequence in the World Cup. Beckham featured in nine of the qualifying matches – with all but one of these appearances seeing him arrive from the substitutes' bench. An Achilles injury, sustained when playing for Milan in March 2010, prevented Beckham from becoming the first English player to participate in the finals of four World Cups. Beckham still travelled to South Africa with the England party for the finals, acting as liaison between management and players. Following the tournament, Capello announced the end of Beckham's England career, after 115 matches in which he had scored 17 goals.

David and Victoria became parents to a fourth child, a girl named Harper Seven, born on July 10 2011. Within a few months, Harper was joining her mother and brothers in the stands, as David played for LA Galaxy. The club won the Major League Soccer title in November, beating Houston Dynamo 1-0 in the deciding match. At the start of 2012, LA Galaxy announced Beckham had signed a new two year contract with the club. Beckham, now aged 36, had made clear his aim to appear in the 2012 Olympics, for Team GB. The best of his playing days were behind him, but David Beckham remained one of the most famous, and fascinating, personalities in football.

12 Lionel Messi: The Atomic Flea

Lionel Messi follows in the footsteps of Alfredo Di Stefano and Diego Maradona, as an Argentinian who ranks among the greatest players in the history of football. Messi has secured his worldwide reputation at a relatively young age, winning a third Ballon D'Or at the start of 2012, aged just 24. Messi is a prolific goalscorer, amazing dribbler, and great passer, with tremendous vision. The ability to elude opponents with his energy, combined with a diminutive physique, has led to Messi being nicknamed "the Atomic Flea". He was born at Rosario, into a family that emigrated from Italy to Argentina a century earlier, on June 24 1987 – three days before the opening of a Copa America tournament in his homeland. Messi made an early start as a footballer, joining the Grandoli club, where his father, Jorge (who worked in a steel factory) was a coach, at the age of just five. He moved to the youth set up at Newell's Old Boys, also based in Rosario, in 1995. Messi's football future was plunged into doubt when, aged 11, he was diagnosed with a growth hormone deficiency. River Plate had considered taking on Messi, but were deterred by the cost of treatment.

News of Messi's talent travelled, via relatives living in Catalonia, to Barcelona, and he was offered a trial with the club. Carles Rexach, a former Spanish international who was part of the management team at Barcelona, offered Messi a contract written on a paper napkin – lacking proper paper at the time. The outcome was that Lionel, and his father, went to live in Spain, with the player joining the youth set-up at Barcelona, and the club paying for his medical treatment. Messi progressed through the youth and reserve teams at Barcelona, from 2000 to 2004, and reached a height of 5 foot 6 inches, the same as Maradona. Messi, who had made his first team debut in a friendly against Porto the previous year, first appeared for Barcelona in La Liga in 2004, against Espanol, when he was aged 17. Further appearances followed over the next few months, for a Barcelona team which won the Spanish title at the end of the 2004-05 season.

Messi's ability was also appreciated in his homeland. He found a place in the Argentina youth team in 2004, and starred as they won the World Youth Championship of 2005. Messi was quickly selected for the full squad, but his debut for Argentina was not a success, as he was sent off just two minutes after arriving as a substitute against Hungary, in August 2005. During the following months, Messi played three times for his country in the closing stages of a successful World Cup qualifying campaign. Ironically Messi obtained Spanish citizenship in September 2005, to go alongside his being an Argentinian. The added nationality strengthened Messi's chances of a regular place in the Barcelona first team – with the Spanish league having placed restrictions on the fielding of non-Spanish nationals. Messi now signed a new contract, pledging himself to remain at Barcelona until 2014.

Messi missed the latter part of the 2005-06 domestic season with an injury, sustained in an encounter with Chelsea, in the Champions League. His participation was enough, however, to gain two medals, as Barcelona retained the Spanish league, and beat Arsenal 2-1 in the Champions League Final. He recovered in time to appear several times for Argentina in the World Cup finals during the Summer of 2006, and scored his first goal in a full international, after arriving as a substitute, in the 6-0 win against Serbia-Montenegro. Messi was, however, left watching from the bench as Argentina met Germany, the host nation, in the Quarter Finals. The match was drawn 1-1, after extra time, following which Argentina lost on penalties. A year later, Messi played for Argentina in the Copa America of 2007, with the competition being staged in Venezuela for the first time. Argentina reached the Final, but lost 3-0 to Brazil.

In August 2006, Barcelona won the Spanish Super Cup, with Messi appearing in the victory against Espanol. Barcelona did not win any further trophies in either 2006-07 or 2007-08, and Messi missed a significant number of games, due to injury, in each season. Playing against Getafe, in the Spanish Cup Semi Finals, during April 2007, Messi scored a brilliant solo goal, that was strikingly similar to Maradona's second goal against England in the 1986 World Cup. Barcelona won the match 5-2 but in the return leg, with Messi not playing, Getafe won 4-0, to take the tie on aggregate. A year later Barcelona were eliminated by Manchester United in a Champions League Semi Final. In the Summer of 2008, Messi played for the Argentina team that won the football Gold medal at the Beijing Olympics. Messi scored in victories against Ivory Coast and the Netherlands, following which Argentina beat Brazil 3-0 in the Semi Finals, and Nigeria 1-0 in the Final.

Frank Rijkaard, who had been coach of Barcelona for five years, was replaced in 2008 by Pep Guardiola. The short fallow period for Barcelona ended in spectacular style during 2009. The club won the

Spanish league, finishing nine points clear of runners-up Real Madrid, who they beat 6-2 at the Bernabeu late in the season. Barcelona also won the Spanish Cup, beating Athletic Bilbao 4-1 in the Final, with Messi on the scoresheet. In the Champions League, a reverse of the previous season's Semi Final outcome saw Barcelona beat Manchester United 2-0 in the Final, staged in Rome, with Messi scoring the second goal with a finely directed header. Messi was the leading scorer in the 2008-09 Champions League, with nine goals. At the start of the 2009-10 season, Barcelona beat Athletic Bilbao in the Spanish Super Cup, and Shakhtar Donetsk in the European Super Cup. In December, Barcelona participated in the Club World Cup, and beat Estudiantes de La Plata 2-1 in the Final, with Messi scoring the winning goal during extra time. This was the first time that Barcelona had won the world championship (after being runners-up in 1992 and 2006). Barcelona had won all six of the trophies for which they had competed in the calendar year of 2009 – an amazing achievement.

A few months later, Messi scored all four goals as Barcelona beat Arsenal 4-1 in the second leg of a Champions League Quarter Final, following a 2-2 draw in the first match. Barcelona's defence of the title ended with defeat against Internazionale in the Semi Finals, but Messi was the tournament's top scorer, with eight goals. Barcelona retained the Spanish league title in 2010, and also won the Spanish Super Cup that year. Messi was a regular member of the Argentina team during the qualifiers for the 2010 World Cup, a campaign during which Diego Maradona became the coach. Ahead of the finals, held in South Africa, there was much anticipation of Messi being one of the stars of this World Cup. He was certainly very active, creating many openings for himself and team mates, but Argentina did not live up to their billing as potential champions. Messi was unable to score in a campaign that ended with a 4-0 defeat against Germany, in the Quarter Finals.

Barcelona had another meeting with Arsenal in the Champions League during the 2010-11 season. After losing 2-1 at the Emirates Stadium, Barcelona won 3-1 at home, with Messi scoring twice, to take the tie. Barcelona eliminated Real Madrid in a bad-tempered Semi Final, which was temporarily lifted by a brilliant solo goal from Messi at the Bernabeu. Barcelona also pipped their closest rivals to win the Spanish league, but Real Madrid won a meeting between the two teams in the Spanish Cup Final. The Champions League Final saw another meeting between Barcelona and Manchester United, two years on from that in 2009. United had the advantage of playing at Wembley, but Barcelona won 3-1, with a tremendous performance. Prior to the match, the British media hyped the supposed rival claims of Messi and Wayne Rooney to be the greatest footballer in the world. Both of them scored in the match but, for the second time in three seasons, Messi eclipsed Rooney in the Final. Messi, with 12 goals, was also the competition's leading scorer for a third successive season. Across the 2010-11 season, Messi had scored an amazing 53 goals in 55 matches for Barcelona.

Proof that Messi was fallible arrived at the Copa America in the Summer of 2011, as he failed to score any goals, despite Argentina being the host nation. Messi did find the net in a penalty contest against Uruguay in the Quarter Finals, but Argentina lost this, and Uruguay went on to take the title. There was a growing debate about the contrast between Messi's performances in club football and an apparent shortfall at international level. Alejandro Sabella, the national coach, defended the player by saying: "Messi is the best player in the world. He plays extraordinarily well for Barcelona so then when he plays just well for Argentina it seems like he is underperforming". Argentina had also struggled with the disruption caused by several changes of coach. Six years on from his international debut, Messi had played under five coaches – Jose Pekerman, Alfio Basile, Diego Maradona, Sergio Batista, and Alejandro Sabella.

At the start of the 2011-12 domestic season, Messi was back on target, scoring for Barcelona as they defeated Real Madrid in the Spanish Super Cup, and Porto in the European Super Cup. The Autumn saw Argentina start their campaign for the 2014 World Cup, with a qualifying group requiring the team to play 16 matches, surrounded by long-haul flights between South America and Europe for most of the players, in search of a hop across the border to Brazil. In December Messi travelled with Barcelona to Japan, where they regained the Club World Cup, beating Santos 4-0 in the Final, with Messi scoring twice. Messi was a prolific scorer for Barcelona this season, and notched five goals as an amazing personal performance inspired a 7-1 demolition of Bayer Leverkusen, in the Champions League, during March 2012.

Away from the football pitch, Messi is a quiet, even shy, personality, whose main focus is relaxation with his family. In 2007 he inaugurated the Leo Messi Foundation, a charity supporting children with health and education. Through this organisation Messi has been able to organise for children from Argentina to receive advanced medical treatment in Spain, something he benefitted from as a youngster. Messi also works with Unicef, having been appointed as one of their ambassadors in 2010. At the start of 2012 *Time* magazine featured a major profile of Messi, built around an interview with the player. When asked about the development of his skills, Messi generously acknowledged the guidance of other people: "Year after year, I've grown, improved. I was lucky to start very young and always have very good colleagues around me as I was coming up, and this has helped me and how I play. With Guardiola, I learned to play tactically, which is what I most needed, what my game needed. From the tactical point of view, it's been about knowing how to stop to think on the field when we don't have the ball. And that makes us better when we have it". Messi also demonstrated the dedication that has been a great factor in his success, saying "I always thought I wanted to play professionally, and I always knew that to do that I'd have to make a lot of sacrifices. I made sacrifices by leaving Argentina, leaving my family to start a new life. I changed my friends, my people. Everything. But everything I did, I did for football, to achieve my dream. That's why I didn't go out partying, or a lot of other things". Other players were asked their opinion of Messi, and Osvaldo Ardiles, who won the World Cup with Argentina in 1978, was glowing in his praise. "I think he's certainly the best player of his generation. And I definitely believe not only that but he's the best player in the history of football. To be perfectly honest, I thought I would never encounter anybody in the same league because Diego was a genius. One of the reasons I think Messi is better than Maradona and Pele is evolution. People before Pele were running 5,000 / 6,000 metres. Now they are running 9,000 metres. Now players eat better, train better, the pitches are better. So this is why I believe Messi is the very best ever". In the ever-more commercial world of football, Messi had certainly made his mark in one respect. In 2010 a survey by *France Football* showed Lionel Messi had replaced David Beckham as the highest paid player on Planet Football, with estimated annual earnings of £29,600,000.

Other Books by Andrew Godsell

A History of the Conservative Party

A critical history of the Conservative Party, from its formation through to the premiership of Margaret Thatcher. The record of the Conservatives in government and Parliament is surveyed, along with the organisation and outlook of the party. This radical interpretation of its subject was the first critical history of the Conservative Party ever published, filling a notable omission in British political literature. Throwing original light on nineteenth and twentieth century politics, the book offers telling observations on many famous figures including Robert Peel, Benjamin Disraeli, Lord Salisbury, Andrew Bonar Law, Stanley Baldwin, Neville Chamberlain, Harold Macmillan, and Edward Heath. The book received approving comments from Neil Kinnock, Ken Livingstone, Larry Whitty, and Ted Honderich.

"Staunch Labour supporter Andrew Godsell has published his first book – an account of the Tory Party from 1830 to the present day". *Aldershot News*

The World Cup

The history of the first sixty years of the world's greatest football competition. The development of the World Cup is traced, from humble beginnings in 1930, through to the amazing festival of Italia '90. Compelling narrative combines with detailed statistics of every match. Featuring winning teams from Brazil (inspired by Pele), Argentina (led by Diego Maradona), England (captained by Bobby Moore), Uruguay, Italy, and West Germany, the text gives due space to heroic outsiders, such as North Korea and Cameroon, who have added drama to the competition. Besides favourable reviews in several publications, the book was praised by the Football Association, India's National Centre for Sports Documentation and Research, and the Zaire Football Federation.

"A book about the World Cup that makes interesting reading. A well-documented account of past competitions with additional comments on the most memorable features of them". *FIFA News*
"A 563 page historical tome". *World Soccer*
"Plenty of fascinating stories connected with the world's greatest sporting event. If you want all the facts, this is the one for you". *Shields Gazette*
"Besides the statistics of both the qualifiers and finals, the book contains a detailed description of each of the fourteen World Cups". *kicker*
"A massive book. It has all the results from the first competition onwards and will be a statistician's dream for all those interested in the world's greatest tournament". *Match*

Europe United: A History of the European Cup / Champions League

The most detailed history available of the first fifty years of the premier club football tournament. Narrative and statistics are blended with biographical sketches of players and managers, plus other features, linking the competition to the wider context. This encyclopaedic study covers the development of tactics, controversies on and off the pitch, plus the growing influence of commercialism. Extensive quotations from participants illuminate events, and the book is enhanced by photographs, spanning half a century of the beautiful game.

"Celebrating 50 years of Europe's top club competition". *Four Four Two*

"Bible for European Cup. A statistician's dream". *Southern Daily Echo*

"Definitive history of European Cup / Champions League. Lots of information and stories. Highly recommended". *Amazon*

"The tale from early beginnings through to the English dominated era of the late 1970s / early 1980s, and the glitz that is the Champions League today". *BBC*

"A superb book. A lavishly illustrated season-by-season history of the competition". *Hampshire Chronicle*

"The entire history of the event is captured by Andrew Godsell, with both his words and the many photographs bringing the memories flooding back". *Romsey Advertiser*

"Lifelong football fan scores with latest book". *Fleet Mail*

"This gives every result recorded in the competition and includes more statistics than you could shake a stick at". *Independent*

Legends of British History

A panoramic survey of themes in our national history, and their contemporary relevance. The narrative stretches from the origin of Stonehenge, five thousand years ago, to political controversies in the twenty first century. The centrepiece is a challenging investigation of the facts behind the legends of King Arthur. Other chapters include original interpretations of the lives of Boadicea, Ethelred the Unready, King Canute, Richard the Lionheart, Samuel Pepys, and George III. The foundation of the monarchy is explained, along with the ideals of the Peasants' Revolt and the Christmas truce, plus the enduring significance of the cults of Saint George and Saint Swithin. Combining profound events with amusing trivia, this kaleidoscope of stories and images is a thoroughly entertaining popular history.

"Andrew Godsell's narrative brings all the best points of each story to the fore, with flair and humour. Godsell applies his own ideas and conclusions without losing the vital facts of each legendary tale". *Amazon*

Fifteen Minutes of Fame

Fifteen Minutes of Fame is a satirical commentary on contemporary society. The book celebrates the cult of celebrity, the wonders of everyday experience, and lots in between. Variety is the spice of life, as Andrew Godsell (with pen in hand and tongue in cheek) explores diverse subjects, combining lots of fact with interludes of fiction. He plays the roles of writer, family man, public servant, and English eccentric, as he wanders through literature, history, politics, sport, music, and television. The author communicates an enthusiasm for story-telling that might be obsessive. Godsell visits John Noakes, discusses football with Bryan Robson, and succeeds in out-witting Anne Robinson on *Weakest Link*.

"Refreshing and inspirational. Andrew Godsell has a positive attitude and the ability to laugh at himself. A colourful storybook full of everyday situations (and some not so everyday) that we can all relate to on some level. A light-hearted and fun read". *Amazon*

Printed in Great Britain
by Amazon